NOBODY CARES

ESSAYS

ANNE T. DONAHUE

Published by ECW Press
665 Gerrard Street East
Toronto, Ontario, Canada, M4M 1Y2
416-694-3348 / info@ecwpress.com

Editors: Crissy Calhoun and Jen Knoch
Cover design: Natalie Olsen / Kisscut design
Cover embroidery: Jessica Albert

To the best of her abilities, the author has related experiences, places, people, and organizations from her memories of them. In order to protect the privacy of others, she has, in some instances, changed the names of certain people and details of events and places.

Library and Archives Canada
Cataloguing in Publication

Donahue, Anne T., author
Nobody cares / Anne T. Donahue.

Issued in print and electronic formats.
ISBN 978-1-77041-423-5 (softcover).
ALSO ISSUED AS: 978-1-77305-259-5 (ePUB),
978-1-77305-260-1 (PDF)

1. Canadian essays (English)—21st century.
2. Canadian wit and humor (English)—21st century.
I. TITLE.

PS8607.06247N63 2018   C814'.6
C2018-902553-0   C2018-902554-9

The publication of *Nobody Cares* has been generously supported by the Canada Council for the Arts, which last year invested $153 million to bring the arts to Canadians throughout the country, and by the Government of Canada through the Canada Book Fund. *Nous remercions le Conseil des arts du Canada de son soutien. L'an dernier, le Conseil a investi 153 millions de dollars pour mettre de l'art dans la vie des Canadiennes et des Canadiens de tout le pays. Ce livre est financé en partie par le gouvernement du Canada.* We also acknowledge the support of the Ontario Arts Council (OAC), an agency of the Government of Ontario, which last year funded 1,737 individual artists and 1,095 organizations in 223 communities across Ontario for a total of $52.1 million, and the contribution of the Government of Ontario through the Ontario Book Publishing Tax Credit and the Ontario Media Development Corporation.

ONTARIO ARTS COUNCIL
CONSEIL DES ARTS DE L'ONTARIO
an Ontario government agency
un organisme du gouvernement de l'Ontario

Ontario
Ontario Media Development Corporation

Canada Council for the Arts

Conseil des Arts du Canada

Canada

PRINTED AND BOUND IN CANADA   PRINTING: NORECOB 5 4 3 2 1

MIX
Paper from responsible sources
FSC
www.fsc.org   FSC® C103560

To my mom and dad, who have kept
me alive in a trillion ways.

INTRODUCTION

I've never been a patient person. At my best and worst, I'm relentless and calculating and exhausting in my ambition, abandoning the "timing is everything" mantra for all-caps outbursts about fish and chips on Twitter. I plan and plot, obsessing over hypotheticals and replaying scenes from *The Godfather* in my head. I'm consumed by the variables I imagine I have to conquer to achieve the thing I might eventually want, and I throw myself into work, believing that channeling my energy into something productive will bring me closer to my goal of the moment — or, more specifically, prove to the universe that I'm ready for whatever the fuck I think will solve everything.

In January 2014, I wrote my first book. I didn't have a book deal, and my agent only asked for a short proposal, but because I couldn't do anything low-key if I tried, I wrote an entire book of essays about growing up alongside the internet.

And that manuscript was fine. It was okay. Between us, it was average at best. It wasn't the worst thing I've ever written (see: a blog I deleted years ago), but I would still rather break into your home and pour my beloved basic-bitch #PSL on your laptop than let any living person read it. I wanted a book deal more than I wanted anything else in the world, and I was willing to write millions of words if it meant I'd get one.

But nobody wanted that book then, and nobody wanted it a year later when my agent and I shopped it around for the second time. Nobody wanted the other book we proposed after that, and nobody wanted the book I had a phone meeting with an editor about either. In short, nobody wanted my books. Which was a problem because I wanted to be famous for writing them. After all, without a highly publicized bidding war between publishers for my stunning debut, how could I tell people I'd written a book — or, more importantly, invite them to my expensive and shrimp ring–themed book launch party? How could I prove that I, Anne T. Donahue, was important — or at least important enough to call myself an "author." Because that's what books are for, and how life and self-esteem work. Please buy me a present, I was — and am — in no way delusional.

In *Tiny Beautiful Things*, Cheryl Strayed reminds a reader that the act of writing books and book deals are not one and the same: "one is the art you create by writing like a motherfucker for a long time [and] the other is the thing the marketplace decides to do with your creation." My gut dropped when I read that line. I wasn't thinking about the art. I wanted the marketplace to recognize my importance and to convince everybody else of it too. Instead, the marketplace and the universe told me to go fuck myself.

Had that first book been snatched up when I was desperate for it, I would've forever been attached to 200-odd pages that operated solely and exclusively as a personal thirst vessel. I would've wagered my happiness on party RSVPs and industry feedback (kill me) and whether or not That Cool Guy From Whatever City Is Hip Right Now thought I was finally worthy of conversation with him. You can't escape your fears by cloaking yourself in the praise of strangers, and nobody else can save you from your worst incarnation.

When I first started my weekly newsletter, *That's What She Said*, my thirst was palpable. Each instalment included links to my work and not much else, and it existed to prove that I was in demand and busy, and *why couldn't everyone see how important I was?* Perhaps understandably, it died very quickly. Partially because nobody gave a shit, but especially because it was very boring to write.

Then in late 2015, I revved it back up again. I wanted to write without worrying about editors' feedback or about being professional. I wanted to write what I wished someone would say to me when I was in the midst of a misery marathon or taking up residence in the bell jar. I wrote about my fuck-ups, fears, and real, human feelings (gross), and dove into events and experiences that weren't gold star–worthy. In it, I was vulnerable, angry, and messy AF, but it felt good to write about life as an often-horrifying shitshow instead of what it looked like through an Instagram filter. For the first time since I'd started writing, I stopped trying to show everybody how great I was and focused on the merits of being a person unfinished. I began trying to work out my issues and feelings in real time and chose to learn as I went. Quickly, the newsletter became the place I could be me and sound like me and write like me and share with the world all the very best Leonardo DiCaprio GIFs the internet has to offer. I was finally happy just to be there. And for the first time in years, I didn't give a shit about being important.

Which is a relief because I'm not. None of us are. Nobody's looking at us, nobody cares — everybody's obsessed with their own Thing. Most of the time we're all just trying our best. And sometimes we fail and other times we don't, but we're sure as shit not better than anybody else before or after the fact. If you can look at your life and feel confident that you're doing something you love and giving it all you've got, I think that's enough. Especially since not even a tidal wave of third-party congratulations will make you feel better if you don't already like where you're at. No amount of RSVPs, no parties, no Cool Guys From Whatever City Is Hip Right Now's adulations. No book deals. You are always left with yourself.

And it turned out people liked my messy-ass self. Including (and somewhat ironically), two book editors who reached out to my agent. So, I've tried to keep toning down my quest to prove how special I am, because I'm not. And to care that much about being famous or world-renowned is exhausting. It's a waste of time and energy. Yet even while typing that sentence, I know I'm still battling. My tightrope walk between anxiety-fueled work binges and genuine hustle, between thirst and a healthy amount of ambition, is a balance I still navigate — daily. And I'm so used to it at this point, I think I'd miss it if it went.

Which is the funny thing about self-acceptance. When you begin to embrace your fuck-ups and anxieties and insecurities and even the most calculating and ambitious and *Godfather*-like parts of yourself, you end up writing a book that wouldn't exist without them.

ANXIETY, YOU LYING BITCH

Some are born anxious, some achieve anxiety, and some have anxiety thrust upon them. I am lucky enough to have been blessed with all three.

Ten years ago, I would have never admitted this essential truth about me. When I began my romance with anxiety, I thought it was all a phase; that stress wouldn't manifest itself in my life (or in my stomach) forever and that, like all youthful dalliances, I would grow out of it — in the same way I grew out of wanting to be Lauren Conrad or marry Benedict Cumberbatch.

With every anxiety attack or anxiety-induced stomach cramp or inability to digest a meal properly, I told myself that it would all get better. That I could "beat" it by self-medicating with booze and sleep aids, or by denying it existed entirely, or by making myself small enough that it might miss me. Because anxiety is a liar, it convinced me that I was the only one it ever visited. It'd whisper its toxic nonsense to me when I was too stressed to question my relentless mental narrative. It kept me pinned down by quietly insisting that if I ever opened up about it, I'd be all alone.

There were certainly signs that anxiety would become A Thing as I grew up: I cried every day in first grade because I missed my mom. I couldn't stay overnight at a friend's without assuming that something bad would happen to my parents unless I was home. I couldn't fall asleep unless my mom promised there'd be no burglars or fires and that she'd check on me every ten minutes "just in case." In middle school, I developed an irrational fear of tornadoes (despite never having seen one) that morphed into a teen and twentysomething fear of food poisoning. (I wouldn't eat meat at a restaurant, ever.) And then I failed a math class, and anxiety spiraled me into a full-on existential crisis.

When I think about that math-defined summer, almost every moment is defined by what I can now identify as severe anxiety: by all-consuming destructive monologues and all-encompassing worries and refusals to acknowledge that what I was feeling wasn't the product of me being a failure, but of my brain being a liar. I'd get anxious about going out, about eating, about having to pretend I was the same person I'd been a few months prior. I'd curl up on my bed on weekends instead of going out, crying because I was afraid to eat dinner since I hadn't been able to digest anything properly in weeks. I'd sob in front of repeated screenings of *Sense and Sensibility*, unable to articulate to my parents what was happening to me or why I was feeling the way I was. And, because anxiety spreads as well as it lies, it began manifesting about work, about friends' birthdays, about my own birthday, about ordering from a restaurant menu.

Anxiety followed me when I changed jobs, during my first year of university, and throughout the following autumn and winter. It hung around when I started to drink more, when I started to drink less, and when I got sober once and for all and was forced to process life without numbness. It would hover over me for days before finally swooping in to convince me that I was failing, that I was weak, that I was alone. It would worsen when I tried to push it down. It thrived in the dark and in my solitude, and the longer I kept it there, the more anxious I became.

Well into 2015, I kept chiding myself for not being better — for not yet outsmarting the narratives that made me feel small and trapped and afraid. So, fueled by comparison with the people around me who seemed to have their lives under control, I threw myself into self-improvement: I decided I needed to commit to being bigger and better, doing more, being more, being smarter, being more involved, less thirsty, more enthusiastic, busier, more relaxed, and, and, and. Perfect, perfect, perfect.

And anxiety clapped back.

One summer evening, my friend Nicole and I had plans to see a movie, and for the first time in my life I was early. I waited for her near the concession stand and scrolled through Twitter while trying to take deep breaths because I'd been feeling out of sorts all afternoon. I'd felt inexplicably rushed on the way over, overemotional when cut off by another driver, and I'd begun to fixate on where we should go for dinner later, convinced that my diva stomach could handle only bread. I was so lost in my what-if narrative that when three guys approached and began chatting me up, I didn't have time to put my mask back on. And now I was trying to dodge conversation starters from a trio of bros who'd opened by telling me to smile more.

Angry and annoyed and hyperaware of how outnumbered I was, I felt my cheeks and palms getting hot, but I was shivering. My stomach was going to fall out of my body, and my legs felt like I'd just run up several dozen flights of stairs. I knew I had to get to the bathroom before I threw up or passed out or projectile wept all over everybody. I mumbled my excuses and texted Nicole to meet me in the bathroom when she got there. I stood over the sink with my eyes closed, breathing in and out, in and out, in and out until she showed up. She was kind in not acknowledging the obviousness of my meltdown.

The next day, I made an appointment with my GP, assuming I'd be prescribed anti-anxiety medications. But he declined. Had I been actively working through my anxiety with my therapist (I hadn't) or doing any exercise (I wasn't), he might have. Instead, he suggested we start by me talking (and breathing) through it.

Which is a much longer road than a paragraph in a book — talking to my therapist was not one conversation that led to me overhauling and retraining my brain. Instead, it is and was a long, tiring, and frustrating work in progress. To this day, I'm still anxious, it still manifests physically, and I still actively worry about what to eat before going anyplace with a questionable bathroom. I'm simply learning how to keep anxiety in a guest role instead of as my co-lead.

I've found ways to quiet my anxiety, to balance my work and the rest of my life, to take breaths, to say no to plans. I've learned that no one will die if I need to reschedule, and that Jessica Jones is onto something when she closes her eyes and recalls the street names of her childhood neighborhood. I've learned to keep track of my plans by writing them down, by asking friends if we can do dinner at someone's apartment instead of at a restaurant if I'm not feeling well. I've stopped going to parties I never wanted to attend in the first place. I leave when I want. I've also learned that anxiety isn't indicative of weakness, but a symptom of being a living human person. It's also an ever-evolving creature you have to constantly outwit to keep it lurking and not thriving. For the most part, I've learned to do a good job of it. Then there are weeks when I feel like I'm back at square one. But, like the bags under my eyes, I consider my anxiety a badge of life experience. Or at least proof that my brain is still mine.

And my life isn't over because I'm open about it. Pretending was exhausting. When I finally began testing the mental health waters by opening up to friends about how I was actually feeling, my revelation wasn't greeted with shame or pity, but with most of my friends admitting the same. I've yet to meet a person who's never felt anxious or sick or overwhelmed. (And if I do, I will assume they are sociopathic.) Which has made it way easier to say what's happening as it happens, instead of excusing myself to a movie theatre bathroom where I'd try to remember how to breathe in a silent panic.

Today, I went to the drugstore after my anxious stomach insisted I give it as much Pepto Bismol as possible. And there, in an oversized sweat suit with flat hair and arms full of drugs and saltines, I ran into someone I hadn't spoken to in about eight years. She looked great. She was fit and tanned and picking up diapers for her kids, looking like my hometown equivalent of Reese Witherspoon's character in *Big Little Lies*. Me, I was pale and blotchy, my eyebrows weren't filled in, and my face had broken out because adult acne is real. Then, within seconds of saying how good it was to see her, I accidentally dropped everything I was holding as she very kindly said, "You look great too!"

Picking up my grab bag of anti-nauseants, I abandoned all remaining fucks and said, "No, I don't — but I'm for sure shitting my way to my bikini body!"

She laughed. The cashier laughed. And the people around me in line laughed, and not out of pity, but because *who hasn't?* At some point, even the coolest, hippest, prettiest, hottest, richest, most together, all-powerful people have needed to take Imodium, all while desperately trying to keep their shit together.

Sometimes literally, sometimes not.

IN CASE OF EMERGENCY

There's this moment in *Happy Valley* that I think about all the time. Catherine (the series' main character) walks down the street and shouts, "WHAT A SHIT WEEK!" And boy oh boy, what a slogan for what feels like most weeks.

Here is what most of us already know in the year of our Lord 2018: for a very long time, everything has been feeling scary and bad. Everyone's feelings and emotions are heightened. Most of us are walking the line between cynicism and feeling absolutely bananas, sensitive to the point of wanting to strike down anyone who disagrees about how disgusting cilantro is. (It is extremely gross!!!) Me, I have stuffed my feelings somewhere near my spleen. Mainly because I have no idea where my spleen even IS, so I assume I will just forget about having emotions at all, and I can just continue on with my life without doing a lot of processing. Every terrible thing necessitates an "Of course this is happening right now," and all of us are very tired.

So let's acknowledge that.

Also, let's acknowledge that right now, in this moment, in this second, you are living and breathing and moving through the misery marathon with the rest of us. This is something you can tell yourself to keep on keeping on when you're starting to feel like you are just about to fall off the planet. You are ON this planet, you fucking freak (I love you), and on this planet you shall stay.

So you're feeling like an anxious mess? Let's get you centered.

Are you breathing? Please breathe. I'm not kidding. I want you to just sit there for a second, and I want you to breathe in and breathe out and take your time and concentrate *only on doing this*. Tell any other thought to fuck off. This is your time to fill your lungs with air. A cool thing. Fuck off, everything else.

Are you drinking water? Drink some water. Jesus. Look, we've all lived on the fumes of caffeine and sleep deprivation while forgetting to drink water because we are idiots. If you're me, you'll experience a beautiful anxiety attack spurred on by running your body into the ground and chasing a Venti Something™ with another Venti Something™. Not a hot look, and not a terrific feeling. So drink some water. Water's great! It's boring as fuck, but that's why carbonation exists.

Have you eaten? You have to eat something. Even if your stomach is staging a coup, have a banana or some crackers. You need something in your bod, dude. You don't need to eat a meal. Just snack it up! Give yourself some fuel. (Also if your stomach does what mine does, start with the BRAT diet: bananas, rice, applesauce, toast. Then work your way up. It's fine! You're okay! Also: Imodium and Pepto Bismol are helpful choices if you're in a situation where you would rather walk into the ocean — and poop there — than use the bathroom right now.)

Are you eating what you're craving? My new M.O. is literally to eat anything I'm craving because I figure there's a reason. Fuck it. (Ed. note: We feel it is our responsibility to add that this might be ill-advised since Anne has the flu, like, 78% of the time.) Most of the time, it's avocado rolls. Often, it's all-dressed chips. Once it was a Cherry Coke. Life is short; eat the thing you would like to eat. Enjoy the goddamn candy you can't stop thinking about. Make some brownies. Eat some cabbage. Yesterday I popped frozen appetizers into the oven and ate them all by myself for dinner.

When was the last time you went outside? I'm not going to tell you to hike, because I would rather die than go on a hike (or do most activities), but I will say that a second outside can be a nice break from staring at your computer and screaming "WHY!!!!!!!" Put your feet on the concrete or grass, and take some breaths, and look at the sky and at the trees or the cars or the driveway or the deck, and think about what you're doing: you are standing outside. That is it. That is what you are doing. Look around and name the shit around you. "I am on the driveway. The car across the street is brown. There is a bird chirping." Keep it simple. Remind yourself how big the world is and how, in this particular second, you are whole and breathing and this is the only thing you need to do right now.

Can you take a second to walk around the block or sit outside, sipping some tea? Is that possible? If not, can you do it tonight? I am asking you this, but also I am asking myself because typing this made me realize I've been cooped up for about 29,428,525 days and "driving someplace" is an accurate descriptor for my only non-indoor activity.

What are you watching? Is it comforting? I don't have the bandwidth to give a fuck about anything not comforting to me most of the time. I know that's "uncultured," but also I don't care because who are you, person challenging me? I want to watch *Veep* before bed because it makes me laugh, and I want to watch true crime documentaries, and I want to watch British actors in terrific costumes battling through emotions they weren't even aware they had. That's all. I'm tired. Find your comforting shit. Build your mental fort and hang out there.

Are you hate-reading anything? STOP THIS NOW. You don't have the time for this, what are you doing? (Especially if it's this book. Please don't hate-read my book. Burn it for kindling, but don't you dare keep reading it.) Are you hate-following anyone? Cut them out of your life.

Do you have boundaries? Bask in those boundaries. Fuck saying yes to things you don't want to do. Oh my *Lord*, you do not have the time for that. Can I tell you what makes me anxious on top of my existing anxiousness? Thinking, "Shit, now I have to go to [THIS THING I WOULD RATHER SLIP INTO A COMA THAN ATTEND]." And you know what? No. Nope! No thanks. No one is ever cooler or more successful because they went to that one party at that girl they hate's house that one time. They are usually just annoyed they didn't make dinner plans with a friend they actually like.

Do you have someone to talk to? Talk to them. A pal, a parent, a therapist — whomever. They may not have a solution to your problems, but don't underestimate how validating it is to have someone just to listen. It's okay to be like, "Wow, I am feeling feelings about things that are happening in my world." Articulate your thoughts. They're valid! Expressing your feelings can help you understand them better, even if your first instinct is to deny that you have feelings at all.

Do you believe you can get through it? "It" being life? Because guess what: you can. You can because you don't have a choice. Everything may be shitty right now, but you know what? Everything has always been shitty. There has always been a shitstorm upon us. And, as with shitstorms of yore, you will prevail. You will get through it, and you will help other people through theirs, and you have to believe that — or just repeat this until you do. Actively pep talk yourself. You have been through your share of shit, and this is just another share.

Then it will end and there will be another wave, and you will have to remind yourself again that this is old hat: you've done it before, and you'll do it again because you are a tough mother-fucker.

Surviving various catastrophes is hard and terrible, but this is how it works. So thank your brain and body for keeping you going and drink some water and take some breaths and eat a banana. Everything may feel like (and may actually be) the worst, but if it's going to get better, we need each and every one of us in fighting form.

I'LL READ
YOUR CARDS

In June 1999, I was the recipient of St. Elizabeth Catholic School's Christian Leadership Award. (Please hold your applause.) And that meant that at my eighth-grade graduation, I got a plaque, I posed for pictures, and I basked in the glow of being my elementary school's equivalent of Miss Congeniality.

I was 13 and I believed in God. I'd never thought not to. My parents were Catholic, and I loved and trusted them, so I'd never had reason to doubt what they taught me. I'd gone to elementary school with the same 60-odd kids since kinder-garten, and year after year we'd studied our religion with the same seriousness as spelling or math. I said prayers before bed (thus perfecting my imitation of a Precious Moments figurine) and took distance-ed catechism courses on top of my Catholic school curriculum for added grace. I was still young enough to believe that faith and fact were interchangeable — and that a Christian Leadership Award was cool.

It was the same year that my classmates and I were confirmed, continuing the long-standing Catholic tradition of pledging our eternal allegiance to the Church before we got old enough to question it. We took additional names (mine is Michaela), donned red robes, and ultimately made our parents proud with our public displays of Catholic-sanctioned affection.

I took home the plaque, but my mom was the true Christian leader. As a little girl, she'd wanted to become a nun until the convent said she'd make a better wife and mother. So, like a small-town Ontario version of Maria von Trapp herself, she climbed a new mountain and, after she met my dad in the church choir, my parents dated, got married, and then welcomed me — Anne Theresa Donahue — a little over a year after their wedding.

My mom's dedication to Catholicism became my own. Because my parents were both volunteers in our parish, most of my childhood was spent going with them to choir practices or council meetings or the annual penny sales. (Where, for the record, you could buy raffle tickets for a penny and bid on everything from bath kits to homemade quilts. One year, I ran the penny sale tuck shop and was the queen of chips and soda, and, to this day, I strive for that level of power.)

But while some of it was fun (tuck shop queen!), most of it was incredibly boring — and inescapable since, as an only child, I went wherever my parents did. As they tallied the

Sunday collection or played music at endless masses, I killed time in the parish rectory where the priests lived. Sometimes I had access to their snacks and cable TV, but most of the time I'd be stuck reading in the parish office, where my mom worked as a bookkeeper and later as church secretary.

So as an increasingly bored 11-year-old in desperate need of attention and praise, I became an altar server. I started training on a snowy November day and started serving proudly the following summer, psyched I'd have somewhere to show off my mushroom cut and Dr Pepper Lip Smackers. I was desperate to make church friends. Our parish was in another part of town, so I never saw anybody I knew from school, especially not the boy I had a crush on. Fortunately, most altar servers *were* boys, and I decided to fall in love with all of them. (It wasn't until after puberty that I clued in that they'd all have rather died than date me.) But the thing about serving is that it gets old. Mainly because *you* get old, and you begin to look tragically out of place as a teenager standing amongst children. I leveled up to doing readings at mass, but by the time I was 14, a certified Christian Leader and confirmed, even the glory of reciting the Bible at the pulpit wasn't enough. So I started going to the same church as my school friends, which meant at least my school crush would finally see me in my Sunday best. (Even if he never seemed particularly dazzled by my sweater sets.)

But it was too little too late. High school made me desperate to distance myself from the Anne who'd so proudly worn her safe and rule-abiding vanilla crown. I had begun to realize that no amount of Catholic guilt could spiritually, emotionally, or mentally tie me to Catholicism outside of my parents' connection to it. So I started to aggressively question my parents about their devotion and resent them for subjecting me to a belief system I felt I'd never willingly subscribed to. I tried not to feel my mom's hurt when I insulted what she held so dearly; I used her maxim that anything worth believing is also worth questioning against her.

My mom, though always soft-spoken, willing to compromise, and a staunch opponent of strict discipline (I used to ask her to ground me so I could skip parties I didn't feel like going to), wasn't ready to relinquish me to complete godlessness. She made me go to mass on Saturday nights if I wanted to sleep in on Sunday mornings. I still had to attend services, but I could wear whatever I wanted — "church wardrobe" be damned — so I used the communion line as a runway for my pleather pants and dramatic sighs.

But all of it only made me angrier. I hated church, I hated going, and I hated how much of my life had been eaten up by something I had never had any real interest in. But the priests were our family friends, and most of them had treated me like a granddaughter my whole childhood, so announcing how much I hated the world they'd devoted their lives to seemed unnecessarily hurtful — even to angsty teen me. My mom, however, was not granted the same humane treatment. Young and emotional and unable to articulate the full scope of my resentment, I unleashed my fury on her when we were alone, and continued to be business as usual around clergy, family friends, and anybody I wanted to impress.

Part of my façade as a nondegenerate was continuing to

go to confession. For most of my teen years, our priest was an old Polish man whom my uncle had nicknamed Cousin Vinny (his demeanor was surprisingly similar to Joe Pesci's) and who'd seen some shit in WWII, believe me. He wasn't particularly friendly to strangers, but the more he warmed up to you, the funnier and more sarcastic he was. I thought he was great: he didn't seem to care about being approachable in any way, was laissez-faire about church rules, and when I'd go to confession, we'd usually just chit-chat. Once, I told him how my friends and I had smashed mailboxes, and he just laughed. (Likely because we both knew I'd end up doing it again.) He made going through the motions of Catholicism easy, but he wasn't always there.

One Sunday when I was 15, I went to church and found a visiting priest in place of our regular one. The man was old and, from what I'd gleaned from his half-screamed sermon, a little eccentric, but I still waited my turn for the confessional. The space was well lit — more like a conference room than the standard-issue, as-seen-on-TV, suffering-in-stained-glass Catholic vibe — but the windows' blinds were drawn when I walked in and sat next to the priest.

"Father, forgive me for I have sinned," I started. "My last confession was . . ." I paused, trying to seem pensive, ". . . a few weeks ago."

He nodded solemnly.

I began rattling off the list of whatever I thought was "bad" at 15: I'd yelled at my mom, or I'd lied about how much money I'd spent at the mall. I confessed to hating someone at school (who, in retrospect, likely deserved it).

"And is there anything else?" he asked.

"I do have a question, Father."

I'd been chatting on ICQ with a senior at high school who was trying to convince me to hook up with him. After years of being taught that premarital sex was a sin, I couldn't shake my Catholic fear of disapproval. What constituted sex? I figured that this conveniently visiting priest could help me draw necessary lines in the sand without my having to ask Father Vinny.

I sat up straight and looked directly ahead at the heavy oak door, determined to ask but not comfortable enough to look a messenger of God in the face as I did.

"So, sex," I said with purpose, channeling the confidence I normally reserved for class presentations on Canadian history. "What is sex, according to the Catholic Church? Like, is it sex-sex? Or is it blow jobs? What about hand jobs? Or . . . What about getting off if you do stuff with clothes on?"

I was proud that I'd gotten the question out — what maturity! I sat still, my hands primly on my lap, and refused to fidget. If I was grown up enough to ask a strange priest about sex, I was most certainly grown up enough to keep making that high school senior think I was seriously considering having it one day. Maybe even with him.

But there was no reply. After he hadn't answered for what seemed like several hours, I looked over at him. His head was bowed down, but he must have heard me move. "Hm," he said. "All of these are good questions, but there's a lineup of people waiting. Why don't you go outside, say three Hail Marys as penance, and come back inside for a talk when you see everyone's left."

"Okay, sounds good," I said, as if closing a business deal. "Thank you, Father."

I walked out, smiled apologetically (and yet knowingly, for I was special) to the people waiting, and sat in a nearby pew, reveling in the knowledge that I was finally an adult, that I was so advanced as a *person*, I had compelled a visiting priest to have a one-on-one conversation with me about the realities of sex in our modern times. I was going to get answers. I couldn't wait until everybody left.

A few praying stragglers remained in the pews, but eventually the confessional line cleared. It was time to go back inside and talk like adults. I walked back in, closed the door, and took my seat next to the priest, who still didn't look directly at me. But this time, knowing we'd already broken the ice, I sat beaming.

"Now," he began slowly, his head down again. "When you were asking me those questions, I had a boner."

Time stopped. The air was sucked out of what now seemed like a dim, glorified closet. I felt cold and hot and sick at the same time. I slouched, losing my business bitch composure and shrinking from his words and my stupidity and how young I suddenly felt. Worse, I felt guilty, like I'd invited this. I felt the same way I had when my sixth grade teacher had rested his crotch on the corners of girls' desks, or the way I did when my science teacher put his hands on my shoulders and rested his chin on my head. But this was those feelings on steroids — the word "boner" lingered in the room.

"I want you to know," he continued calmly, as if lecturing

a petulant child, "that your words affect men. You need to be responsible for the things you say to them."

I held my breath and tried not to move for fear of doing anything else provocative. I stared down at my outfit — a crochet top worn over a baby-blue tank and a black skirt — and assumed that, like my words, they were responsible for this.

"Right," I said too quickly, too loudly, desperate to leave. "No, yes. You're right. I got it. I'm sorry."

I wanted to get out of that room, and I wanted to erase the knowledge that I'd been in close proximity to the erection of that old-ass man. But I also wanted to know that I wasn't cheap and dirty — that what this priest had said was weird and wrong, and that my growing cocktail of guilt and shame and disappointment and anger wasn't my doing. I wanted to know that, despite what he told me, it wasn't my fault.

My parents, despite their Catholic affinities, have always been safe people to talk about sex with. (Nobody in our family has time for anything but facts, and for that I am grateful.) Which is why I told them the truth the moment I got into their car, idling in the parking lot waiting for me.

"So I asked Father What's-His-Name about sex and what's a sin," I started. "And he told me he had boner? And that I shouldn't talk about sex like that with men, because I can do that to them? I don't know." I laughed, trying to play down the situation while waiting for confirmation that what had happened wasn't fine. They looked at each other, then looked back at me in the rearview mirror.

"What?" my mom said.

"Just that —" I immediately regretted saying anything. "I

have to be careful with the way I talk to men . . . ?" I wanted the feeling to go away, and this wasn't helping.

Still no answer from the front seat as I saw my mom look at my dad again, then back at me, and then back at my dad, who kept his eyes on the road. As my mom opened her mouth to finally say something, I cut her off.

"Whatever." I sunk into my familiar terrain of teen angst and faked disinterest. "I don't want to talk about it."

And I didn't. After telling my best friend, who gave the requisite best friend answer of "Gross," I didn't talk about it with anybody. I was as horrified at the man as I was at the institution, so I focused on getting out: out of the confessional, out of the religion, out of my Christian Leader image, and out from under my parents' idea of who I should be spiritually.

I switched from Catholic school to public school (no more mandatory school masses and religion classes), and when I started working part time, my shifts made it impossible to go to church every Sunday. So, I kept chipping away: soon I only attended mass if I was volunteering with the choir kids or on major holidays. Then finally, after insisting on wearing a miniskirt and Von Dutch hat to a Good Friday service, I was free. My mom resigned herself to the fact that I wasn't a Catholic anymore.

But I didn't award my mom the same level of under-standing. The thing about having a personal revelation is that, when you're high on the momentum of figuring your shit out, it's easy to decide that anyone who disagrees with you is wrong. And the thing about *that* is that it's the best way to become the most insufferable version of yourself, morphing into a brand of "Well, you've probably never even heard of that band." For years after I stopped going to church, I made it my personal mission to make my mom feel terrible about her involvement with it. I lectured her about Catholic Church scandals, yelled about the dangers of a boys' club, and asked how she could consider herself a feminist while subscribing to a religion that governs the bodies of women.

At no point did I pause to hear her answers, her explanations, or her own experiences. To me, her religion, her allegiance to an institution that hurt people — including her own daughter, her own flesh and blood — made her into a two-dimensional caricature, and I didn't give a fuck. To me, she was one of the congregation sheep, blindly believing everything a guy in a robe said. I never listened when she'd tell me her devotion wasn't about the business of the Church or the Vatican, or that she was spiritual, or that you can challenge norms from the inside. She told me she saw the same problems I did, but that singing at church — which she did every Sunday — brought her joy. I made her cry a lot, wanting her to feel as frustrated and angry with the institution as I did. I wanted her to be angry at the Church's misogyny, at its homophobia, at its abuse of power, and at the individuals who gave an entire religion a bad name. I railed against the Church's intolerance, failing to see my own as I shamed my mother for being true to herself.

Around the same time that Catholicism first began to lose its shine for me, I started reading tarot cards. My friend Alanna and I would hang out at her house, teaching ourselves the Celtic Cross spread and asking a million different questions about whether or not we were destined to be with the guys we liked (we were not) before finding new, roundabout ways of asking the same questions all over again. We called it "playing tarot" and basked in the ritual of snack-eating and heart-to-hearts that came with hours spent dissecting what our cards meant, or why one came up so frequently.

But that was just part of the appeal: where Catholicism was built on following a distinct set of rules (laid out by men), tarot left room for personal interpretation and self-exploration. Church was a place where I sat silently, being told what to do. Nights spent tarot reading with Alanna led to conversations about our goals, our insecurities, and the patterns we fell into. It made me feel like I could be in control of my life and make sense of my own experience.

I remember coming home and triumphantly telling my mom about tarot and seeing the mix of shock and confusion on her face. I pushed down the guilt that came with seeing her disappointment in me and smugly began dropping tarot references as a means of lording my newfound spirituality over her. The kid who'd once ratted out her friends for bringing a Wiccan book to school was now a 16-year-old heathen and loving it.

Tarot nights were soon replaced by bars, clubs, and drunkenness. Actively believing in something like magic means you have to be vulnerable and, even scarier, be yourself. Instead, I'd chosen cynicism and hardness, that precious emotional armor. I became a character in my own story, as opposed to being who I really was.

A few weeks before I turned 30, one of my best friends from university, Judith, was getting married. She'd reintroduced me to magic and spirituality when we'd first met, but I hadn't then been ready to open up to it. The night before her wedding, her best friends got together in her hotel room: we ate pizza and watched *Practical Magic* and christened her new deck of tarot cards. Judith asked us each to take one. We were supposed to sleep with our card under our pillow and then the next day, explain to each other what the card meant to us. Pulling the card felt like going home. The ritual felt like a celebration, like action instead of passive observance. I didn't feel like a dummy for subscribing to a belief or exposed by being vulnerable. I felt the opposite of what I used to feel when I was cooped up in church on a Sunday, wondering when the priest's words would spark something in me. Within weeks, I'd ordered a deck of my own.

About two years later, my mom and I had a heart-to-heart about Catholicism and tarot and crystals and intuition and spirits and all the things we couldn't talk about until I'd finally begun to grow up, to shut up, and to confront so much of what was making me angry. To reexamine my definition of spirituality, my feelings about religion.

After I stopped being Catholic, she never lectured me or yelled at me, nor did she try to force me back into the religion when she realized I was serious about leaving the faith. And eventually, she apologized for not reacting to the priest's harassment the way I'd needed her to, explaining that she'd been just as shocked and surprised as I had and didn't know what to do. She apologized for assuming church would mean to me what it meant to her, and I apologized for picking fights in a quest to assign blame to her after so many years spent being angry.

That night, decked out in a sweat suit (me) and a matching PJ set (her), we sat on her bedroom floor, where she finally let me read her cards. With the room bright and cozy and my favorite crystals laid out around us, she sipped her nighttime tea as I pulled for her three cards: the Daughter of Cups, the Empress, and the Mother of Pentacles. To her, they represented the creativity she finds in church singing and the power it gives her, as well as her emotional strength and her ability to listen. And she didn't argue with them, even though tarot intentionally leaves space to do so. She was taking the time to understand what I believed in, and the cards reminded me that I'd found my own spiritual path because of her.

We apologized for years. Now I can yell about series like *The Keepers*, and she will agree with my points and remind me of what a character in *Spotlight* says about subscribing to the belief, not the institution — which, I've finally learned, my mom doesn't represent. After everything, I finally saw that she and I were so much more alike than I'd ever realized.

I still hate church. I'm still angry at Catholicism. I still want to set buildings ablaze whenever I think about the centuries of institutionalized bullshit that's defined that religion — and continues today. I only go to mass for weddings and funerals, and I do not take communion. That is me, and those are my beliefs, and I'm not going to impose them on you. Even if I think pulling a few tarot cards will make you see things a bit more clearly.

Instead, I just try to channel my mom, who taught me more about patience and understanding than the Catholic Church ever did.

NEAR, FAR, WHEREVER YOU ARE

I don't remember where I was when I first saw him, but I remember when he became *Him* and not just some guy. I mean, sure, he'd been around. I knew his name. I knew his work, his friends, his social circle. I told myself I wasn't interested, that I was better than everyone who looked his way, who complimented his eyes or the way his bangs fell into them. I was my own hero, the main character of my own story. I didn't need to be rescued or die as proof of my devotion to my teen husband.

Leonardo DiCaprio was a haircut and a smile. He was fancy slacks and David Blaine. He wished he could be the love of my life. And somehow, his wish came true.

They say timing is everything. Too young to see *Romeo*

+ *Juliet* upon its release at 11, I considered myself old enough for *Titanic* at 12 — except that I wasn't. Thanks to my parents' penchant for rules, I was forbidden from seeing the PG-13 cinematic masterpiece until I turned that very age, so I spent the entirety of seventh grade pining.

One moment I knew his name, and the next? His face, age, filmography, zodiac sign, hometown, hobbies, former girlfriends, current girlfriend, mentors, Academy Award nominations, proximity to Tobey Maguire, and that his friends called him "Noodle." He seemed so hardworking and loyal to his mother, so seasoned, and yet, thanks to his complete lack of facial hair, so approachable. The clips of *Titanic* I saw on television and in the "My Heart Will Go On" video also implied that he — like Jack Dawson — was sweet and sincere, willing to talk a woman out of a terrible relationship and draw her nude without trying anything inappropriate. So, clearly, he respected women. He loved women. And, being a man who'd yet to meet this specific woman (me), he had what every boy in my seventh- and eighth-grade classes didn't: absolutely no idea how uncool I really was.

When I finally saw *Titanic*, rented on VHS three days after my 13th birthday, I came to understand my soul mate on a deeper level: the way he flicked the hair from his brow, the way he ditched Fabrizio for a woman he'd met four times. I noticed how willing he was to give up his place on that wardrobe door, and I appreciated how clearly sex was meaningful and emotional for him. I may have not yet understood the technicalities of what exactly was happening between Jack and Rose in the back of that Rolls Royce (or whose hand it was slamming against the window), but I knew no one could possibly act *that* well: when it came to dramatizing the throes of passion, the boy had me shook. And that was so much more appealing than the guys in my class whose go-to jokes were about jerking off on the bus.

But I still wasn't completely delusional. I knew I'd have to wait years to meet and begin dating Leo. I knew that for us to meet as working actors (an important life goal), I still had to be discovered at the mall or looking mysterious while waiting for my parents to pick me up outside the movie theater. I knew that our road to love would be long and storied, and while he'd be refreshed by my Claire Danes in *Romeo + Juliet*–like naïveté, he still had to date the string of women he'd eventually leave for me, the love of his life. I knew the best love stories had plot twists because that's how movies worked.

It helped that a boy in my class had Leo's haircut and that he was tall, misunderstood, and rebellious enough that he also wouldn't have fit in at a first-class dinner party. The year before, he'd burned down a townhouse, and in eighth grade, he'd thrown a desk across the classroom when our teacher had caught him taking too much Ritalin. In short, he was perfect. And, unlike Leo, he knew who I was. He'd be my stand-in, my practice round. He'd be the first of many men I'd horrify my parents with, which would hopefully encourage my mom to forbid me from seeing him, the way Rose's mom forbade her from seeing Jack anymore. (I just needed to find a corset she could lace up for me while she did it.) So, I began speaking to him regularly. And, because our class was small and most people got along, he began speaking to me back. So I assumed that we were days from recreating Rose and Jack's iconic sex scene, and that someone's hand would eventually come to imply . . . whatever it was implying. I began to wonder if in his spare time he drew nude women, or if there was a chance our class would go on a boat trip that would end in disaster (although I, of course, would survive). I knew for a fact that his and Leo's names both starting with an "L" was a sign.

But the more I talked to Leo 2.0, the more I began to like him, less because of his DiCaprio-esque qualities and more because I really liked him. He thought I was funny. He told me how frustrating his dad could be. He looked at me when I was speaking to him. Between the winter and spring, our friend groups began to merge, and he and I began talking on the phone almost every night. And while there was a small smudge on our record — when he asked out my best friend and they dated for three weeks (prompting me to listen to "On My Own" from *Les Misérables* on repeat, usually while crying) — he told me he liked me despite this fact, and our conversations continued. By May, I'd even begun to wonder whether Leo really would be jealous, like I'd been telling myself he'd be. By June, I'd begun planning how I'd describe this tragic love story to Leo.

The rest of my teen years were defined by young men who weren't Leo. Because his *Man in the Iron Mask* wig embarrassed me. And as cute as he looked in *Catch Me If You Can*, *Gangs of New York* was a real downer and caused tension between me and my friends when I wouldn't let them talk through it. Like so many young loves, Leo and I had clearly grown up and grown apart. He was a serious actor. And I was serious about having no interest in seeing *Blood Diamond*.

They say that when you stop showing interest in someone, they know. That when you've forged your own path and created a life without them, they emerge from wherever they were hiding to try to lure you back. The afternoon I saw *The Great Gatsby*, I was overtired, PMSing, and had a headache. I retreated to the darkness of the movie theatre as a means of escaping my phone and parents and responsibilities for a blessed two hours, and I looked forward to losing myself in twenties-era costumes and that Lana Del Rey song about youth and beauty. Then I saw him.

By 2013, I was old enough to understand how similar Leo and I were not. I knew he loved models, loved being spotted with models, and loved introducing models to his vast collection of cargo pants and newsboy hats. At some point, I'd realized he was kind of The Worst. Sure, he wanted to save the environment, but he also used to call his friends the Pussy Posse. Frankly, I reminded myself, we'd have more in common if he'd burned down a townhouse.

But, like the green light in *Gatsby*, his eyes begged me to return to him. And as the movie went on (and on, and on — it wasn't good), he channeled the manic pixie dream boy magic of Jack Dawson and seemed free of the onus he'd put on himself over the last decade to prove to us he was a Master Thespian. He seemed — as if he were attending a party in third class — like he was having fun.

Which I can only assume was because he knew I'd be sitting there watching him. Yes, years had passed since the universe had brought us together, but true love transcends time and reason. It cancels out Oscar-baiting, erases a legacy of disappointments and heartbreak and ill-advised headwear, and brings you back to the moment your eyes met and he said those fateful words to you: "I'm the king of the world!"

I hate that line, but if I can love him while he's saying it, that means it's real. And while we haven't met face-to-face yet, and by his standards I'm too old to date him, repeated screenings of *Titanic* have taught me that none of that matters. True love doesn't reason; real love doesn't make sense. When two people are meant to be, life and love will find a way.

At least they will if he follows me back on Twitter. And stops wearing cargo shorts.

WORK, BITCH

In 1992, in celebration of both my seventh birthday and the new bank within walking distance of our house, my parents helped me open my first bank account and agreed to give me two dollars a week to tidy my room and "learn to save."

Three months later, I'd saved up enough for my first Barbie, and on a drizzly Saturday, we made our way to Kmart and invested in her Hawaiian Fun™ self. Girlfriend wore a two-piece bathing suit and came with pineapple-flavored lip balm, and everything else I owned was immediately trash in comparison.

Barbie (constantly renamed depending on what TV or movie character I liked best) quickly became my best friend. I prized her, I outfitted her, and — as all true blues do — soon realized she needed more than just me as a pal to live a full life. So I began to save again. My doll needed someone she could trade clothes with and discuss the politics of life in plastic (it's fantastic). And I wanted a Barbie with brown hair. The point of saving was clearly to spend.

But over time, my needs evolved: from Barbie dolls to Beanie Babies to cassettes to CDs to the entirety of the Lip Smackers cosmetic collection. My $10/week allowance (shout-out to inflation) was holding me back from living like Cher Horowitz. I needed some real income, and I needed it fast.

Money was freedom. My family didn't have a lot of it, which made me want it even more. Fortunately for me, I was of the last generation adults entrusted their children to, a phenomenon known as "babysitting." While I wasn't nearly popular enough to found my own club, I still managed to book myself solid every weekend.

A million nights of my pre-and-early-teen life were spent lounging on near-strangers' couches, eating their chips while ensuring their children were also safe and breathing upstairs, all in exchange for enough money to buy a new, discounted camouflage-print top. For years, I rotated amongst families, a weekend fixture at many houses whose pantries I either respected or resented. While most of my classmates' weekends were spent doing "cool" things, mine were even cooler thanks to Blockbuster rentals, unlimited soft drinks, and the $5/hour that competed with actual minimum wage.

But if from ages 12 to 14 responsibility reigned, 15 ushered in a brand new era. Work existed only to fund weekends of drinking, buying going-out clothes, and drinking too much while wearing our going-out clothes. The busier I got, the less I wanted to work "so hard" for $5/hour. So I began looking for work that paid more.

And so I began working in fast food.

The McDonald's I worked at was across the street from where I lived, directly beside the parking lot where most of my friends and I hung out. A few days before Christmas, I filled out an application on a whim and, despite having no customer service experience, I found myself working alongside girls from my first high school, a guy I had a crush on, and a slew of fellow youths who liked making as many inappropriate jokes as I did. For $6.40/hour, I was in heaven.

And for a few precious months, it stayed that way. I loved my 3.5 hour shifts, I loved working my way up to the drive-thru window, and I loved the way our 50% store discount allowed me to create my own meals in which I combined burger sauce and mayonnaise as chicken nugget dip. But then the novelty began wearing off.

It wasn't long after I first put on my pleated uniform pants, golf shirt, and visor that I learned two very important lessons:

1. I am very, *very* good at upselling pies.
2. I am very bad at doing anything I don't care about.

I could distract angry guests with jokes, I could crack up a dad in a minivan, but night duties like cleaning the grease off the fry cart or topping up the milkshake machine were doomed to failure. Mainly because I failed to even try. I was busy flirting with the guy who liked my impression of Chandler Bing, and it's hard to look sexy in tapered trousers while spilling sweetened milk all over them.

My incompetence understandably became a problem: I talked too much, I leaned too hard ("If you have time to lean, you have time to clean"), and, at one point, I had my shirt untucked. But, like Wolverine, I'm a survivor. For every write-up or verbal warning I accumulated, I'd one-up my own pie sales record and prove that if I really wanted to apply myself, I could be marginally employable.

By the time my first anniversary approached, I'd become less a shining paragon of pastry sales and more one of the most annoying people in the restaurant. I began waxing poetic about how little I needed my job (not true) and how over the whole "scene" I was (I'm so sorry), and I began bragging about my impending interview at a major clothing chain. I confidently gave a shift away on the day of the interview, threw on my most business-appropriate logo T-shirt, and prepared myself to meet destiny.

As I sat in the small fluorescent-lit staff room interviewing with hopes of becoming a bona fide Old Navy sales associate (with a reasonable discount), I got too bold. Too comfortable.

"And do you like cleaning?" my lovely and kind interviewer asked. "Because a big part of the job would be keeping your section clean."

I laughed like Jeff Goldblum introducing chaos theory in *Jurassic Park*. "Oh," I said, leaning back in my folding chair, "I *love* cleaning." A pause. "I love all that shit."

I didn't get a call back.

Thanks to a friend with an in, I ended up with a part-time job at a bargain discount shoe outlet. I took to ICQ and announced the second phase of my career: retail. Which lasted 15 years.

I didn't complain right away. Now earning $7/hour, I made peace with the fact that reorganizing shoe displays was the glamorous step I'd need to take to earn cash shift responsibilities. I could roll in wearing knockoff Doc Martens and Dickies pants and lean for hours, discussing hangovers with my coworkers on the sales floor or smoking outside on the front curb if there weren't any customers around.

But the sheen wore off within weeks. On top of our store only providing us with two three-hour-long CDs to play over the course of the year, I realized that I didn't like selling shoes nearly as much as I liked buying them. So I did what I'd come to do best: stop trying completely until I abandoned ship altogether.

I'd broken my McDonald's record and lasted a year and a half at the shoe store. It was time to move across the parking lot. An electronics box store hired me at a whopping $8/hour, and soon I was a pair of khaki pants and branded denim button-up away from leaving footwear behind for DVDs, CDs, and video games.

I ruined everything in a week.

One evening, the night before one of my first shifts, I celebrated with a bottle of wine and whatever else my friends' parents had. My equally drunk friends and I took to the streets for a brisk stroll and some casual flashing. I managed to roll my ankle three times before falling down and limping back to our friend's, where I plopped down on the curb, called my dad to pick me up, and cried wine tears until I passed out.

I woke up the next day nauseous and determined to reclaim my dignity and independence. Fueled by the belief that I'd broken a bone, I took a cab to the hospital and limped to the registration desk, convincing myself that my ankle had only begun to feel better because it was somehow getting worse. I had to call in sick for the night.

"Hi," I said to my manager, making sure to sound like I was also fighting off consumption. "I can't come in tonight. I'm [*dramatic pause*] at the hospital."

"Oh," he responded, clearly unmoved by my plight. "Are you sure you can't make it? We don't have anybody to close tonight."

"I am," I said stoically. "It might be serious."

"Okay," he sighed. "Get better."

And I did. Within hours. By the time I was diagnosed with a minor sprain, the excitement of maybe needing a Tensor bandage had given way to an even more important realization: that even though I could totally make it in to work on time, it'd be much more fun to just go to the movies.

High on knowing we were seconds from watching an accented Harrison Ford in *K-19: The Widowmaker*, my friends and I walked into the theatre with the confidence of knowing nothing could possibly go wrong. Which was when I saw my manager.

It's hard to regain passion that never existed, specifically in a professional relationship. A mediocre employee who'd already earned the nickname "Chatty," I was branded the store's weakest link and told by my manager that if I called in sick again, I'd be fired on the spot.

I sat there while he lectured me and smiled while nodding robotically. I'd been lectured and written up in the past, but I'd never actually been fired. I felt like I'd been caught passing a note in class. I felt my heartbeat in my ears. I knew my cheeks were bright pink, and I apologized, scared that I was going to get fired and have to explain to my parents that I was a fuck-up. As if this were the first time I'd acted unprofessionally at work. I swore that I'd never call in sick again. I was always happy to rebel until I got caught.

Less than a month later, I started feeling sick at work. My throat was sore, and my head was pounding, and the crispness of my wrinkled denim began to hurt my skin. I told myself that it was normal for my bones to ache and for the fluorescent lights to be so bright that I had to keep closing my eyes.

I had been handed my fate and would die next to the copy of *Bubble Boy* I was too tired to label. "She loved movies," my family and coworkers would say. My manager would break down. "She was so strong," he'd quietly weep. "She saw *K-19* despite nearly dying."

But death wouldn't come easy. The manager's assistant denied my request to go home to die, believing I was faking — like a better-accessorized version of the Boy Who Cried Wolf.

To survive, I needed to circumvent him — literally. Watching him take laps around the store, I timed out his route and began crawling through the CD and DVD aisles, curling up amongst the understock and resting my eyes before battling the fluorescents again. "You look really sick" became the chorus of my fellow employees. I made peace with the fact that I'd be the first person to die next to a Nickelback display. I heard my manager approaching, but kept my eyes closed. He couldn't fire a dead person, and I was excited for my ghost to haunt him.

"You can go," he said, chuckling. The store was closing in 15 minutes. I looked out into the dark parking lot and saw the headlights of my dad's car waiting for me. I scraped myself off the floor and vowed to burn the store to the ground.

Instead, about three months later, I started work at a steakhouse, where I promised myself I would never make the same amateur mistakes again. If I could care about one thing, it'd be table numbers — well, and shifts that came with complimentary bread.

My first shift was on August 13, 2003 — the day of the massive eastern seaboard blackout. I showed up anyway because I'd learned from *K-19*. The managers asked why I was there and told me to go home. The dawn of a new day.

At 18, my only plans in life were to marry Jimmy Fallon and kiss the server whose chinstrap beard I'd opted to overlook. I didn't care about how naïve and young I seemed to grown-up guests willing to shell out for lobster and steak, nor did I care about how unprofessional I sounded doing impressions of Robert Goulet at the host stand. I cared only about righting the wrongs of my previous job, so I refused to call in sick under any circumstances.

I went to work with no voice, with a migraine, with food poisoning. I went to work when I had fifth-period English, and I went to work on Valentine's Day for a 10-hour shift with only one break to eat the free bread. The day my dad's appendix burst and he nearly died, I rushed into work five minutes after my shift started and apologized profusely, explaining myself to a chorus of "Don't let it happen again."

I wouldn't.

I told myself this is what adults did. That if I forced myself into this industry, I'd force myself into caring about a career.

The thing is, by this point, I did like working. I liked feeling responsible and, since I was flailing in school, like I was actually good at something. And while I may have gotten in trouble for being too casual or greeting adult guests with a loud "Hey, guys!" I thrived when we were busy and the staff was on the verge of implosion. I memorized my table numbers, learned how to properly project wait times, and bonded with the manager everybody else was afraid of. (She was blunt, and I respected that.) I liked feeling near-panicked and under stress. Drunk on this realization, I'd ask to work when it was busiest, thirsting for nights when I'd be the only person at the host stand, stuck doing the jobs of three people, getting high on my newfound sense of purpose and the myth that if I wasn't there, the whole operation would come tumbling down.

I ignored how upset it made me when the owner got angry about me standing up to a group of men who'd sexually harassed me, and I smiled when male servers chose to communicate solely through inappropriate comments about me, my coworkers, and any aspect of our female bodies. Because for the first time since being an adolescent babysitter, I was finally good at a job, and nobody was going to fuck it up for me.

The problem was, I worked at a restaurant. And to succeed

in the restaurant business, you have to not actively hate it. And hate it I did.

Not that I was unique in that hatred. Ask any teen how they feel about their part-time job, and most will tell you that they can't wait to quit. (Ask most adults how they feel about their *full*-time jobs, and many will probably give you a variation of the same thing.) So instead of doing what I tend to do when unhappy (flee), I resigned myself to the fact that all I could aspire to was not wanting to smother myself with complimentary bread whenever I got to work. Five jobs in, I just assumed that regardless of industry, everyone was destined to hate the place they worked.

The first time I hated writing, I was home sick with the flu and had a hard deadline. I lay in bed at my parents' house and started to cry about having chosen a job that hinged on my work ethic and not on set shifts or hourly rates.

One year earlier, I'd finally quit my job as keyholder at American Eagle to focus on writing full time. And despite being ready to leave after four years of balancing registers, making sales goals, and folding jeans, in my sickness haze I couldn't believe I'd once hated a job that let me work with my friends, take structured breaks, and give up my shifts if I was at death's door. I complained to my mom that I didn't know how good I'd had it, that I'd made a mistake venturing down the path of self-employment and self-sufficiency, and I pined for the days I could get paid for hanging out amongst flip-flops, eating snacks. I couldn't believe there'd been a time when I'd hated retail. Especially since, unlike in freelance writing, at least in retail my managers would reassure me of my strengths with employee reviews or overtime shifts. I always knew where I stood, how I could improve, and what I was good at that I'd never thought I would be.

I hated writing again this week. I was tired. I got stitches in my finger. My booster shot made me so sick, I had to call my parents to check in on me. I emailed my editors to ask for an extension on this godforsaken book, and they very kindly and professionally explained that outside of a two-day grace period, I'd committed to the hand-in date. I cursed my stupid decision to be a writer. Writing was the worst, and only an idiot would commit to writing a book in the first place. I wept for how brave I was to keep working despite being gravely ill.

But such is (working) life. I don't know a single person who loves everything about their career all the time because no aspect of life is perfect all the time. No friendship, no relationship, no family dynamic, no outfit, no movie ending. No job.

My serial employment wasn't a straight-ahead "career path," but, aside from funding vital parking-lot parties and baby tee acquisitions, it helped me figure out a lot about how I work (or don't). I learned I needed a job I believed in enough to offset my own restlessness. I learned that I needed fresh challenges and credit for what I do. I learned that I needed a job where I could work for hours on end when inspired, but could also seek solace in a Harrison Ford movie if my brain needed a break. I learned that if confronted by angry strangers, I could stand my ground and say things like "I don't like your tone" (or, most importantly, "never @ me"), and that I was capable of being responsible and could thrive under pressure. And while my jobs taught me that money was important, I learned that no amount of it could make me love a job I hated.

But maybe most importantly, I learned that there's always something else to try. Even if, like teen me, you are trying everybody's patience. Or barely trying at all.

FAILING
UPWARDS

I wasn't ready for college, but my high school teachers and guidance counsellors thought I should be.

There was really only one sanctioned path to follow after high school: post-secondary education led to jobs and opportunities and a bright, sparkly life. Without it, you'd be left stunted, unfulfilled, and generally fucked.

I certainly didn't seem like college material. I'd spent four years of high school dodging deadlines and classes. I failed twelfth grade and had to repeat it. But then I was shaken by the fear that my life would be over before it had begun, so for my second act I swore I'd do better — that despite not connecting to most subjects or knowing what I wanted to do, I'd turn over a new leaf and at least give myself options. I even applied to college — lack of interest in anything it offered be damned — because I didn't think I had a choice.

But between my lust for PG-rated rebellion and my inability to admit how scared I was in the wake of my existing failures, my newfound scholastic fervor didn't last long. Instead, I refocused on social currency, desperate to be accepted and interesting and equal parts unique, badass, and totally cool.

Somehow, I was accepted by a few colleges. I chose the one closest to home and told myself the stakes would be higher when tuition was involved. A career in journalism would be a fresh new page, and I was already the master of reinvention.

The first day was a disaster.

Thanks to the combination of rain, traffic, and my own inability be on time, I was so late for my first class that instead of charging ahead to forge a new life phase, I dejectedly turned the car around miles from campus and came home to cry in the kitchen and call my mom, who urged me to go back and "just see."

And did I ever: I attended all the rest of my classes for the first week, which gave me plenty of time to realize that a life in traditional reporting wasn't for me. But instead of dropping out and getting my money back (or sticking it out to see what I could learn), I readopted my too-cool-for-school persona. I skipped class, didn't hand in assignments, and didn't study for tests because I hated my program. But college professors aren't like high school teachers. They don't want to hear about why you can't make it to a lab or lecture — they just fail you.

So in December, I dropped out and announced plans to work full time at the hardware store I'd been a cashier at for the last couple of months.

It wasn't glamorous, but adulthood didn't seem to be, either. I spent hours ringing in pressure-treated wood and garden soil and was surprised by how much I liked it. I didn't have to be so formal, to seem "ladylike" or grown-up (when I obviously wasn't), and I was shocked at how efficient I could be during busy hours. My supervisors noticed: more hours led to more money and responsibility, and I began working my way up the ladder. Only a few months after leaving college, I was promoted to full-time cash supervisor with benefits and a guaranteed 40 hours per week. And I didn't need a degree to get there.

But within weeks of being promoted, I knew I needed another change, because High School Anne had made a triumphant return: I morphed into an apathetic supervisor and a disastrous customer service associate, and I wielded my power to do absolutely nothing outside of drink coffee in the cash supervisors' office. I talked back to customers, didn't listen to my managers, and certainly didn't deserve to have full-time hours. I was too proud and scared to admit that I needed to step down and sort out my future. So I just came in to work, fucked around, and cried when I didn't think anybody could see me.

What made it sting more was that I'd begun watching my friends start to build their own lives at school, mapping their goals and dreams. I was jealous: their stories of dorm mishaps, test cramming, and roommate debacles overshadowed my tales of contractors I had to yell at, career shoplifters, and the 60-something employee who'd killed himself after getting fired for stealing. I still believed that academia was the only viable way forward, so I saw everything I was doing as proof that I wasn't good enough to make it academically or in general. School was supposed to be the goal, but I hated being there. I was a prisoner of the myth of convention, too scared and sad to begin thinking unconventionally. My life was over, and I would never be happy.

One day, a coworker cut her hand in the lumber department and I handled it quickly and without balking at the blood. Someone joked that I should be a nurse and, desperate for a way forward, desperate to be *anything*, I agreed. That night, I signed up to begin upgrading my high school marks under the belief that they would lead me to the safety of full-time work in a field everyone seemed to admire. And, for the first time in nearly a decade, I was actually really fucking good at school.

Seeing this as my last shot for the type of future my teachers told me to want, I desperately decided to give a shit. I handed my assignments in, put my hand up in class, and threw myself into a realm of academia I never thought I'd be a part of. The summer I was 22, I was only one math credit away from the marks needed to get into my program. For the first time, I began thinking of my future life outside of the confines of my own shortcomings, and began dreaming about my adult self as a nurse (or a nurse practitioner or doctor or surgeon or chief of surgery or superhero — whatever). I bid adieu to insecurity, to anxiety, to wasted potential. I finally had a plan.

And it blew up instantly.

I have never been able to do math. In ninth grade, my math teacher stopped trying to help me (I was beyond help), and in tenth my mom bought me a CD-ROM math program, hoping I'd finally learn to make sense of numbers (it made me cry). I could do math related to money, but having done so well in school over the last few months, I thought I could will myself into destroying calculus. I was a Real Student now, and regressing wasn't an option.

I sat in the front row of that summer school math class, putting up my hand to the groans of students who didn't want to hear me asking the same questions about why x equals y, or where our teacher found the integer, or what the formula meant. I began skipping lunch to stay in and study. I began bringing my math text to work. I'd read and reread my notes before bed. But it wasn't enough: I didn't get how the numbers worked. Two weeks into class, I sat at my desk and looked at the thumb that had begun twitching from stress. I got up and asked my teacher if I should bother staying.

He put down his sandwich and scanned his binder for my name.

"Ah!" he said. "Right now you're sitting at a . . . 35%." His tone had morphed into that of a doctor telling you not only that you're going to die, but that you actually died years ago. "I can't tell you to drop it," he continued. "But it's going to get harder."

We looked at each other. He picked his sandwich back up, and I packed up my bags and left. This failure was new. It existed *despite* my best effort — despite rallying like a mother-fucker to prove how smart and capable I was. This failure was one I should've felt proud of since I'd given it my all, but it felt like a failure of self. *I* felt like a failure. I cried the whole way home.

By the end of the summer, I'd begun telling myself that school would never be for me, that I wasn't good enough or smart enough or driven enough, and that I should keep my dreams to what I knew I was already good at. Even though I had no idea what that was. I'd spent the last few months weeping at the cash register at my new job at American Eagle while fielding questions from my concerned teen coworkers who worried that they were heading down the same path I was. I believed my life would be only as good as it was in that moment.

Despite wanting to do more (maybe write, maybe enter-tain, maybe a combination of both, who knows), I accepted that it would never come to pass, so I quit my retail job and got a job at a bank. Those were the types of numbers I had always understood. And everybody seemed to take bankers seriously.

Unsurprisingly, I was still miserable. And as self-destruction had become my default mode, I became the worst bank employee in the world, wearing the same Old Navy slacks for days at a time or spending hours in a friend's office eating candy. I was the only bank teller to have a −30% sales revenue, which meant this New Future was also a dead end.

One night, I applied to a BA program at university because I figured the situation couldn't get worse. I'd upgraded enough of my high school marks to make the basic requirements, so even if a career in the arts promised no real outcome, those years I'd tried wouldn't be in vain.

Two months later, I was accepted. I vowed that, despite evidence to the contrary, I was capable of achieving the one thing I'd been told by teachers should be my only real goal. Finally, I was going to do what I should've done years ago.

At the start of the semester, I started writing for the school paper. And while I spent my first year making the Dean's List, earning good grades began to pale in comparison to writing about what I loved: movies, TV shows, music, and my opinions about all three. By year's end, I'd begun to feel restless. The more I found out about the careers of artists and writers and people I admired, the more I realized that many hadn't earned a degree. A degree wouldn't guarantee writing jobs or my own TV show after I graduated — which had slowly become my ambition du jour.

My parents didn't fight me on it: neither had gone to university, so both were just anxious for me to find a career that ensured I'd be able to pay bills. If writing could do that, that was fine. (I decided not to tell them how long that usually takes.)

The next year, I dropped out to freelance full-time. And despite the lack of money, the instability, and the politics I'd yet to really understand, I found myself having fun. Which was surprising since I'd found myself on a path defined by uncertainty: the very thing I'd been trying to outmaneuver by throwing myself into college, banking, and that godforsaken math class. I wasn't sure where writing would take me, but I was sure that doing it made me feel alive in a way I hadn't before.

Not that I had the perspective yet to see my past as anything but a dark mark on my abilities. Armed with jokes about my career-path pinballing, I branded myself a failure [*pause for polite laughter*] before anybody else could. My failures still didn't feel like they were my choices. And the last thing I wanted was for anybody else to realize that.

A lot of us are raised with a series of checkboxes we treat like stepping stones to a middle-class dream life: you graduate high school, graduate college, land a fulfilling career, find a spouse, buy a house, have 1.7 kids, and retire in time to spend thousands of dollars on a boat. We're urged to make choices that guarantee our stability or help us save for the future without taking into consideration that stability and a future aren't guarantees, but privileges. We treat life paths as one-size-fits-all options and forget that histories, socioeconomic realities, and individuality make our slanted idea of conformity impossible. There is no one right way to "adult." Sometimes it's earning a degree, sometimes it's making it all the way to Friday.

But these traditional success stories are still inescapable. And even if you're happy after choosing something unconventional, convention still looms and fosters doubt. So in winter of 2016, I went back to school. I registered for a part-time class and believed I could earn a degree while writing full time. Despite having "owned my failure," part of me still wanted to cancel it out. I ignored that I was overworked and stressed, pretending I was Hermione Granger: a type A workaholic with a god complex who couldn't get enough information or knowledge or grades or approval. (All of which is true.) I ignored the voice telling me that I could read books about what I love learning about, and that I didn't want to shell out top dollar for textbooks I'd eventually give away. So I completed one class, got an A, and then dropped out immediately afterwards. I felt like a failure all over again.

But failing is universal. It's a language almost everybody understands. Without slipups and mistakes and doing the wrong things because the right ones still seem so scary, we'd never figure out who we are. Plus, failure's never permanent. It's part of the process, not what defines it.

It takes years to unsubscribe to the myth that success looks a certain way and that the road to it is singular. I'm not sure if I'll ever wear my lack of degree as a badge of honor rather than a chip on my shoulder. But no degree, no job, no person will grant you admission to the rest of your life. There is no one thing that can guarantee success or happiness, and life is so rarely a straight path. Which is a bit terrifying, but also freeing.

So, keep trying until you find something that makes you feel great and capable and happy. You know when you've made the wrong choices. But one of the best things about moving forward is that you can keep checking in until you build a life that looks like your own. Not anybody else's.

THINGS I HAVE
NOT FAILED
(BUT QUIT PROUDLY)

Persistence is a commendable trait. Patience, a virtue. But also? Fuck those things — if I try it and I hate it, I'm not doing it anymore.

I am not a joiner; I am not a teammate. I am bad at collaboration, and I am even worse at sharing the glory. I could pretend that I'm not an adult incarnation of Angelica from *Rugrats*, or I could operate under the guise of honesty and admit that I write best alone because I want all the praise and attention. I will never answer back to a call and response. I am a mule with the personality of another mule who is extraordinarily self-aware. I love not attending events, and I love quitting shit I hate even more. And I started young.

1991: T-BALL

I was the only six-year-old in the world who was bad at T-ball, and I didn't give a fuck. I sat on the bench with my mushroom cut, eyeing everyone playing this idiot sport while making peace with the fact that I'd rather play real baseball or play nothing. (I played nothing.) I got a participant sticker and cursed my classmates. They didn't hear me, because they were playing T-ball.

1991: CRAFT CLUB

Too much wet glue.

1998: PIANO LESSONS

I hated piano lessons. I hated piano lessons so much. I hated piano lessons more than anybody in this world can ever know. There are no words to describe how much I hated piano lessons. But I will use some anyway because that is how books work.

I was very good at piano. I got my grade six, which is a big deal because there are eight grades before you go on to . . . well, what I can only assume is hell. But who cares, because I hated it. I hated my teacher, who raised her voice at me, and I hated her creepy husband, who'd show up to lessons and hit on my mom in his underwear. I hated practicing, I hated playing, I hated theory. I hated that when I bought the *Titanic* sheet music, it sounded nothing like the soundtrack, and I hated that playing Aqua's "Barbie Girl" on piano made it seem like a song you'd hear at a funeral for a person you hated.

My mom and I went to war over piano. She would tell me I had talent; I would tell her I didn't care. She would tell me she wished she could play; I would tell her that I wanted to play outside. Finally, I told her that my piano teacher was bananas, and, after more tears (and a detailed account of the times she'd sworn at me over scales), I was finally free.

1999: MY HIGH SCHOOL'S PRODUCTION OF *OZ!*

A musical based on *The Wizard of Oz* (and not the HBO series). I tried out for the lead, convinced I'd win over my teachers with a rousing rendition of my favorite Shania Twain song.

"Name and song?" they asked.

"ANNE DONAHUE," I stated proudly. "'WHOSE BED [*a pause*] HAVE YOUR BOOTS BEEN UNDER.'"

I did not get the part. And I quickly learned that if I didn't get 100% of the attention at all times, I needed to excuse myself from the production as soon as possible.

2000: TRACK AND FIELD

I lasted five practices before my friend Ashley and I faked injuries and abandoned ship.

2000: CHEERLEADING

Technically, I didn't quit. Technically, Ashley and I were the only two people cut after the first cycle, and technically, it was because we swore too much when we made mistakes. But whatever, I probably would've quit anyway. Who are we kidding?

2003: SCHOOL COUNCIL

I don't remember quitting. In truth, I have absolutely no

recollection of doing anything, in any capacity. Ultimately, my exit from the council's dance committee can be described in the words of John Green: slowly, and then all at once.

2003: JOGGING
I got shin splints. Fuck jogging.

2003: SCRAPBOOKING
I'm too finicky to be crafty. IF IT'S NOT PERFECT, IT'S GARBAGE, WHAT DON'T YOU UNDERSTAND? (And other things I've screamed at a craft store.)

2004: DEBATE
Apparently, arguing and debating aren't the same thing, but I'll argue otherwise.

2005: ROLLERBLADING
I wanted rollerblading to be cool more than anyone ever has, even in the '90s. So my friend Jaimie and I would rollerblade in our jeans and tank tops, covered in self-tanning moisturizer, all while convincing ourselves we were in the Cambridge, Ontario, equivalent of *Laguna Beach*.

But then Jaimie started her full-time summer job, and I wasn't confident enough to rollerblade alone. Now I harshly judge and mock all rollerbladers, of whom I'm secretly, painfully envious.

2005: ACTING
I mean, with my zest (thirst) for recognition (attention), it

makes sense. But no. Acting takes patience. You wait for auditions, you wait for roles, you wait around between takes. And, like writing, you have to work your way up. Acting is hard, and I hated it.

I signed with an agency when I was 19, incorrectly assuming that this meant I was the next Rachel McAdams. I took classes, I earned certificates (that absolutely meant nothing), and I got cast as an extra in a documentary series about a bombing. I played a victim, spent the day in wet flameproof clothing, covered in fake blood and soot. I had zero lines and spent the entirety of the 11-hour shoot on the floor, behind a table. I earned $90, and my acting career ended as soon as I got home. For about four years.

2009: ACTING (AGAIN)

On a warm day in late April, I answered a Craigslist casting call for extras for a movie called *Scott Pilgrim vs. the World*. The casting director said I had the look (I had bangs, and it was a call for "hipster types"), I was given a call time for 1 p.m., and upon arriving at the location (a church basement), I learned my day would last for approximately 12 hours and then start again five hours after that. So, like any logical 24-year-old, I began to cry hysterically and was dismissed in disgust. I walked no less than 3,000 miles to my car, chain smoked the whole time, and — as it began to rain — realized that now I would probably never be friends with Michael Cera. (Unless he's reading this right now. If so, please DM me.)

2009: BEING IN A BAND

"We should be in a band!" is a thing I said to my friend Sam. He, being the human equivalent of a golden retriever, invited me to come over and jam one afternoon. I played the keyboard for 20 minutes, told him I was hungry, we went for breakfast, and we never spoke of our band again.

2009: GUITAR

If you don't have the patience to attend an acting audition, you do not have the patience to build up callouses on your fingers. I just wanted to be Jenny Lewis.

2016: YOGA

I couldn't — and still can't — touch my toes, and the thought of trying to do that in the same space as a bunch of people breathing loudly was as appealing as, well, trying to touch your toes in the same space as a bunch of people breathing loudly. But, in hopes of combating my anxiety a little better, I bought a yoga mat, subscribed to Yoga with Adriene on YouTube, and told myself that this was it: I, Anne T. Donahue, could fucking do this.

And for a while, I did.

It helped that Adriene was so nice. She congratulated me (and only me — not the other million subscribers she had) for showing up, and she wanted me to practice yoga at my own pace. But my own pace was: do it well, do it often, do it exactly like the instructor whose actual career is doing yoga all day, every day. Be perfect or go to hell.

Which is probably why I started to hate it. I'd either push

myself too hard physically or crucify myself for not being relaxed enough.

Then I got the flu, blamed yoga, collapsed on my bed, and stayed there. I rose on the seventh day to look upon my yoga mat as the enemy it was: another symbol of my obsession with being perfect. I stuffed it in the back of my closet until half a year later when, aware that I'd gained weight due to lack of exercise, I figured I'd give it another whirl. I got the flu again days later. Fuck yoga.

But I've since realized that I'm fine with my anxious-ass, can't-touch-my-toes life. In my soul, I am not chill, and I do not want to be calm, and no part of me aspires to Zen. Sure, through yoga I learned to take time for myself, and I learned how to deep-breathe through pain, but the most valuable thing yoga taught me was that I'm not built to be a yogi — and that's the only mantra I need.

For anyone who wants to be a yogi but hears the internal cries of "Oh my God, I hate this so much" from start to finish? Fuck it. Oh man, fuck it all the way back to wherever you bought your mat from. There are other outlets for your energy, other ways to carve out some peace. Nobody here needs to force themselves into downward dog when they'd rather be walking super-fast around the mall.

Which, for the record, might be the one thing I know in my heart I will never, ever quit.

"WHY DON'T YOU DRINK?"

I woke up on a Thursday morning in May and wasn't too sure how I'd gotten home. I'd gone out the night before, and I'd come home by myself — that much I knew. I squinted at the sun coming through my blinds and began to piece it together. I remembered the long drive on the highway and the boredom of the last half hour. I remembered looking across the lanes at the restaurants lining the exits and wishing I could stop at one because I was hungry. I remembered that it wasn't even too late and that I was surprised at how early I'd decided to leave.

I looked over at my nightstand and remembered taking my prescription before bed, chasing that prescription with any sleep-inducing drugstore meds I could find in my nightstand.

I remembered waking up, thirsty and heavy-feeling, chugging some water, and going back to sleep. And then I opened my blinds and remembered that I'd driven myself home.

But despite that revelation — of another drunken hour-long commute, of another morning spent piecing together conversations, people, and places — I didn't want to think about what my life would look like without booze. To think about the nightmare of sober Christmas, sober Easter, sober afternoons. To think about not drinking to write, to hang out, to feel better, to arm myself against real vulnerability. I reminded myself that I'd never done anything too bad, that I didn't get hungover, that I wasn't doing coke or heroin or taking anything #controversial, and that if I was really an alcoholic, I wouldn't have been able to drive home at all. I reminded myself of all the movie characters and friends and family members whose alcoholism had been loud and messy and over-the-top, and I soothed myself with the reminder that I wasn't like them. I lay there trying to convince myself that I was better, that I was stronger, that I was a grown-ass woman making her own grown-ass choices, and that everyone else got drunk, so why couldn't I? I pushed the nagging feeling down, again, along with the feeling that as much as I told myself I was in control of my drinking, I knew I wasn't.

If I chose to stop drinking, I'd have to engage and be present and sit there vulnerably without the lubrication of wine and beer and gin. I'd have to confront reality without liquid courage and confidence, without the built-in excuse that I'd had a few too many. When someone offered me a drink, I'd have to say no.

And then I started to cry.

The first time I got drunk, I was 15 and with two friends from school; I choked down three beers and a glass of whiskey. I dry-heaved once then made it to the party in time to sit on a senior guy's lap. I never came close to throwing up again. So, while I was certainly an annoying young drunk, I told myself that I was still pretty good at it.

My dad's mom drank. I only knew her after she found sobriety, but a lot of my dad's childhood memories involve domestic disputes fueled by too much drinking. Which is likely why I've never seen my dad drunk: for a long time, he avoided drinking altogether. Only a few years ago did he start to have beer, and at the very most he'd doze off after a few of them. And when I drank as a teen, he seemed to either ignore me or fixate on me doing it so young. Compared to his experience, I wasn't an alcoholic — he'd seen a *real* drinker, and I didn't look anything like that.

But the older I got, the more complicated my habit became. I started to drink to fall asleep, to feel confident, to write. I began to drink *well* — I learned how to make sure nobody ever really knew I'd been drinking at all. I drank to feel included, and I drank if it was offered. I drank to break the ice; I drank to spark real talk. I drank to hit on boys, and I drank to justify kissing them. Drinking could open a strange gateway to vulnerability.

I drank because it gave me the illusion of control. I drank to justify intentional fuckery, knowing I could always circumvent real accountability by blaming it on too much of whatever I'd had the night before. I drank because I could escape from my anxiety and my worries and my hang-ups and everything that held me back.

And I drank because I liked it.

Because that's the thing: I liked it. Drinking was my favorite pastime and my costume. For a few solid hours, I got to convince myself (and everybody I met) that I was really much better than my actual self — a shiny, full-color version.

Not that Drunk Me was ever *actually* as charming or as interesting as I convinced myself she was. I knew I was stuck in a persona that annoyed people as often as I entertained them. I'd find myself in the downward spiral of repeating "That's not what I meant" to irritated looks and eye-rolls. I couldn't catapult out of the conversation in which I was justifying driving home despite nearly having fallen down on my way to the car. My morning-after routine became wondering what I'd said and in what tone and who I needed to apologize to. But all of that paled in comparison to the idea of something even more daunting: sober reality.

That morning in May, I accepted I had a drinking problem. And, because movies and TV shows claimed that I couldn't do it alone, I broke character and reached out, emailing a few friends who had stopped drinking to ask how they'd known it was time to get sober. They were honest and warm and understanding and wonderful, offering me their time and support.

And, clearly determined to maintain *some* sense of control, I told myself that outside of admitting my problem, I didn't need help; that, unlike everybody else, I could do it alone. As I began explaining to friends that I was going to stop drinking, I peppered my revelation with promises that I'd still be fun and I'd still go to parties and everything was fine because I was fine, really, promise. And under that claim, two days after deciding to get sober, I went to a party where the alcohol was free and flowing, and every drunk person wanted to know in detail why I wasn't having any. Which is how I learned that the old chestnut about sobriety is true: it really is about taking it one day at a time. Particularly when navigating drunk people who want to know why you aren't drinking.

My first year sober was slow and tedious and I hated it. I remember counting the days to May 8 (my start date), when I could finally celebrate a full year of sobriety. At first, the idea of going that long without liquor seemed impossible. It felt weird to even use the word "sober," as though I was infringing on a term reserved for people who *really* couldn't handle their drinking. (Unlike me, a person in denial about how much I could handle.) I stumbled to answer questions about why I didn't drink, why I couldn't drink, and why I didn't see myself drinking in the future. I'd get defensive if friends asked if I "still wasn't drinking," as though they should understand the severity of my alcoholism despite my never having opened up about it. I'd get nervous the first time anyone had to engage with Sober Anne instead of her wine-wielding counterpart, terrified they'd dislike the person under the mask of too much gin. I'd lead with the acknowledgment that I wasn't drinking before anybody could notice it. I made jokes that alluded to my problem without committing to having one. I clung to control in any way I knew how.

Those first 365 days, I tried to hide my sobriety, to downplay it, all in an effort to make people around me comfortable. Instead of telling them to shut up and be normal, I made it my problem if they felt self-conscious drinking around me; I'd stay too long at parties or at restaurants to prove just how chill Sober Anne was.

I'd reached out to my sober friends, sure, but I felt defensive when they checked in on me, assuming they thought I couldn't take care of myself. So I continued to overcompensate. I was *fine*. I didn't drink anymore, and it was fine. I announced that my problems had stopped when my drinking had.

But, for the first five months after quitting booze, I still took sleep aids and over-the-counter cold medicine to pass out before bed, until I made myself sick by taking too many. *Maybe* my addictive tendencies weren't limited to my zest for things I could drink. Like *maybe* (I learned while working with my therapist) I had broader issues with control and addiction and using substances to dial down my anxiety. And maybe self-medication is a real dangerous way of trying to quiet the noise of a mental health disorder. And maybe alcoholism also runs in the family.

Okay, fine.

As I began to learn more about myself, as I got older, as I got *tired*, the less concerned I became with how other people perceived my sobriety. The more comfortable I got with my sober self, the less I felt compelled to make strangers feel comfortable around me. Because my personal decisions aren't up for public debate. And neither are yours. My sobriety is public knowledge but personal history. I know what brought me to this place, and I've made peace with it. I've come to realize I get to decide who I share details with, or whether or not I feel like suffering fools who forget what a sober person might like to drink at a party. Like getting sober to begin with, the choice is mine. If me not drinking makes somebody feel weird or uncomfortable, that's on them. And if they try to make me feel weird or uncomfortable about it, they can go fuck themself.

Lying in my bed that sunny morning years ago, I never thought I'd get to this point. I never thought that without wine or beer or gin, I'd be able to declare that I do not give a fuck. Or that I'd be able to write about the darkest and most embarrassing parts of my life — or anything — without the help of a shitty merlot.

Getting sober was hard. Being sober *is* hard. I hated being vulnerable and opening myself up to the kindness of people who care about me. (Still hate it, writing this essay was a nightmare.) It took years for me to loosen my grip on the idea that vulnerability meant weakness and accept that it's an important part of growing and changing and challenging ourselves. And the most sobering part of all of it? Those are things that never actually stop.

IT'S CALLED
FASHION, LOOK IT UP

It is a hot day in September, and I am buying a fur coat.

The coat is old, I swear. It's vintage, it's on sale, and it smells like the stale cigarette smoke of a powerful lady. And right now, I need to feel powerful. It's been A Real Time: a series of unfortunate events spurred on by guy stuff and friend stuff and family stuff and exacerbated by my choice to push all of it down instead of asking for help. I try on the coat. I selfie in the coat. And I look at the selfie, and I like the woman who's staring back at me. She is unfuckwithable and terrifying. She is bold, she is confident, she dares you to ask if the fur is real. I feel exactly like the woman I need to be to make it through the next few months.

Clothes are always my safest way to usher in change. Fashion is one of the first ways you get to assert your independence, to show who you are to the world. In eighth grade, I felt like I'd earned my rightful place in young adulthood when I graduated from kid-friendly fleece to the camouflage tank tops and button-ups I swore I saw on Drew Barrymore in *Seventeen*. I was sure my limited-edition Hello Kitty glitter gloss would make my crush notice me, or if I bought bright plaid flared pants, I'd look enough like Tamara from *Breaker High* that a Ryan Gosling look-alike would be totally bewitched by my presence. Of course, my eighth-grade aesthetic was poetic in its tragedy. My favorite outfit was a pair of Adidas pants worn with hiking boots and a Gap bucket hat, and I honestly thought I looked like Kate Winslet in *Titanic* in my self-described "kinda crochet" graduation dress. If my outfit screamed Rose Dawson to my classmates, too, maybe I could conquer the world (or at least the slow dances at my graduation). I was old enough to recognize the power of celebrity fashion, but still young enough to believe that a garment could convincingly make me look like someone else. Because no matter how many bucket hats I owned, deep down I knew I was still only Anne Donahue.

High school called for a rebrand. I swapped out *TGIF* chic for pleather, platforms, and bright polyester halters. I used clothing to broadcast who I hung out with, what music I liked, what movies I saw, and the stores I could afford to shop at. I was convinced new clothes would erase any memory my classmates had of how uncool I'd been, would help them see how adult I finally was. But I was more like a kid playing dress-up.

The runways of high school hallways see more fashion turnover than the bargain rack at Forever 21, and my approach was no exception. One month, I pledged aesthetic allegiance to skate and snowboarding brands to convince hip skater boys that I was cool enough to hang around with them. Weeks later, I poured myself into ill-fitting clubwear to dabble in the all-ages nightlife I assumed Carrie Bradshaw had once lived through. I used brands like American Eagle and Abercrombie to make me feel academic despite knowing I was the opposite, and at one semiformal dance, I layered a bikini top under a tank because I thought it made me look like Kate Bosworth in *Blue Crush*. Shortly after, I dove headfirst into hipsterdom, where I used vintage clothes and novelty accessories as a way of proving how much better I was than everybody. Fashion was the fastest way to pretend I belonged when I was filled with self-doubt. Fashion was the easiest way to hit reboot.

By my late twenties, I'd left behind fashion tribalism, especially as I found myself feeling increasingly anxious, sad, and lost. While I'd technically rebounded after losing control over my job and finances, anxiety was still very much obsessed with me. And, because anxiety is Kathy Bates in *Misery*, it got even worse as I tried to bury it. So I once again played dress-up to try to create an identity outside of who my inner monologue told me I was. I used clothes to dress up as a woman who had her shit together by layering pieces I hoped would mark my first step into becoming a woman who really *did* have her shit together. And it worked.

I started with bags. I began scouring for purses that made me feel like a fancy person and then quickly descended into shoes, which I'd previously dismissed during my years of novelty everything. The clothes I'd accumulated over the previous decade — that I'd bought either to hide in or as part of in-your-face "statement" looks — felt uncomfortable and inauthentic, so I began purging my wardrobe. And when I bought new pieces, they had to be things I felt strong in. Pieces I felt could protect me from my self-doubt and imagined worst-case scenarios.

The same rule applied to makeup — but only after being forced out of my comfort zone. I'd once hidden behind thick black eyeliner and matte red lipstick, but an allergic reaction to old product (gross) forced me to forego my traditional look. So, I started taking new risks, boldly venturing into makeup trends I'd sworn I'd never wear (Black lipstick! No eyeliner at all! Glitter!), and learning that not only was experimentation fun, but it let me express a spectrum of who I was and how I felt. I contained multitudes, and so did my palette. For the first time, I wasn't using makeup to hide, and I wasn't using it to try to seem conventionally pretty or even attractive. My face was a canvas on which to paint, illuminating the best parts of myself while uncovering even more things I liked. And as someone who's always been creative and loud and good at taking risks, I began leaning further into that part of myself, wearing my strengths on my face and daring anyone who had a problem with how I presented myself to say something. Anything.

No one did.

Soon, I began taking the same approach to clothes, using them less as a means of control and more and more as an exploration of who I was and what I was capable of. I finally stopped pushing down my past and resurrected my former selves by amalgamating them through tops, jeans, skirts, and dresses — literally wearing who I was on my sleeves. I mixed and matched vintage, wore platforms, bought silver, gold, and sheer pieces, and picked up what I previously would've told myself I'd never get away with. And as I did that, I began to realize that even my most "embarrassing" looks had served as stepping stones to becoming the woman I finally was. (Even if I wasn't willing to repeat all of them.) I was dressing in a way that appeased my *own* taste, which I'd finally learned to trust.

By my early thirties, I was dressing like a soldier preparing for battle, and my battle garb could be anything from a cheetah-print jacket to jogging pants. Clothes were a source of reckoning and of comfort, serving as the plus-one for any mood or occasion. Yes, I'd sometimes be stifling a panic attack about where I was going, what I was going to eat when I got there, and what if, what if, what if. But by taking the time to plan my uniform — pieces I felt good and strong in, and makeup that complemented those feelings accordingly — I built that sense of control and sense of self. Even when everything felt bad, this was one thing I already knew felt good. Did I feel like a mess? Sometimes. (We all do sometimes.) But if I looked like a mess, it's because I wanted to.

That same September afternoon, I look at the mom jeans and faded T-shirt I'm wearing under the fur coat and realize that even in moments of feeling less than battle-ready, I've learned to wear exactly what I feel I need to. Recently, I've felt as thrown together and tired as that outfit, held together by caffeine and MAC. Before discovering the coat, I caught a glimpse of myself in the mirror and noticed the way I slouched as I rummaged through dress racks. I'd come in to buy clothes I could lose myself in as I figured things out, choosing pieces that would blend into the late summer afternoons and exist just to cover me up while I navigated how I was feeling. I remembered how I'd started the season consciously dressing up, planning outfits instead of slipping into pieces that I could wear easily, and parading each like a personal victory. But over the summer, clothes had become a glorified blanket fort I used to shelter myself while trying to sort out the rest of my life. Then I tried on that coat. And I realized I was ready to morph back into the version of myself who didn't mind being seen.

It's easy to believe that changing your clothes will change your life, but no: they simply change the way you navigate it. With a deliberate approach to fashion, we can dress for the selves we need to be. We use what we've learned in the past to evolve into our next incarnation. We still carry with us the ghosts of the teen who shrouded herself in camouflage or the twenty-something so proud of her distressed denim skirt. Our reasons for how we dress vary depending on what we're going through: we dress to hide, to spark change, to stand out, to feel like we're in control. And all of these reasons are important. But more important still is the sense of power our style choices give us. Because when we wear what we want — casting off the pressure of trends or outside opinions or anything other than our own taste — we curate a collection that reflects who we've decided to show the world.

"That's an amazing coat," the store owner says, catching me trying to snap another selfie. I quickly pretend I'm checking something out on my phone, mortified that my moment relishing a Disney villain aesthetic has been interrupted. "Do you want me to take a picture of you?"

I pause for a second, debating whether or not to own up to my narcissism, whether I'm feeling so unfuckwithable that I'm willing to let someone I hardly know in on how powerful an old mink can be. I glance at myself for a second, wondering what the previous owner of this coat would do, whether I should dial down my enthusiasm for having found a piece I connect to so well.

"Yes, please!" I say, handing over my phone.

After all, clothes are always about who you want to be and how you want the world to see you. And I want everyone to know that I indeed plan to take over the world in this massive fucking coat.

JUST DO
WHAT I SAY

I've learned there's no real difference between me in real
life and the person I am on Twitter or on Instagram or in my
newsletter. I know that I am loud and brassy; I gesticulate
wildly and will pep talk you in your immediate face because
who's better than you? No person, thanks. And I know this
because I got to speak on a panel recently, and no matter how
hard I tried to lean into an indoor, professional tone, I still
couldn't shut up the broad I've become.

So help me, I can't stop talking. And now I can't stop
thinking about it.

Which is something I'm slowly learning to feel fine about.
I've written about self-esteem and about confidence and

about embracing the person you are (versus the person you think you should be), and how liberating it is to say "I AM ON MY OWN TRAJECTORY, BUT THANKS FOR THE FEEDBACK, JK I DO NOT CARE." I know that trying to be another person is doing a disservice not just to yourself, but to the human you're attempting to emulate. And I know that doing this sets us all up to lose because we usually only attempt to emulate a very specific part of a stranger's life, which we've interpreted subjectively. Sitting here, writing this, I tell myself I get it. And sitting there, reading this, you probably think you do too. But then fast-forward to tomorrow, next week, or sometime next month, and I will inevitably find myself caught in a "Why do I always bring up serial killers during small talk?" mental cyclone. And then I will play and replay everything I said and the looks I got and the tone someone used when they said they'd email me, and I'll fixate on all of the worst parts until I find out five months later that nobody but me even remembers having had that conversation at all.

So I'm going to try to defuse that. Because usually when we need a reality check the most, that's when we have the least luck finding it. WELL, QUEST NO MORE, unless you have access to an actual best friend who'll tell you to get with the program. Because I'm here to tell you that what you said wasn't so bad, your voice wasn't too loud, and everybody you spoke with was just relieved you were willing to talk, so they wouldn't have to. But don't take my word for it.

Just kidding, absolutely take it.

Hi.

"Fuuuuck, I cannot believe I said that thing."

Oh shit, what did you say?

"Ugh, just like . . ."

Actually, no. Expand, please. Was it racist?

"What? No."

Sexist?

"No."

Homophobic?

"No."

Transphobic?

"No."

Xenophobic?

"No."

Okay, well, right away, congratulations: you're not an idiot. Otherwise I'd tell you to apologize immediately, take accountability for what you said, donate —

"Yeah, I just said no."

I know, but you could also be lying, so let's get this taken care of. Like I was saying before you interrupted me on my own page: donate to an organization that assists the community you just offended, educate yourself on why what you said was offensive and what led you to feel comfortable saying it, and figure out a way to educate those around you.

"Okay. Well, I didn't say anything along those lines."

Great! So, moving on. You're embarrassed.

"Well, I just said something that came off weird, and I said it in a tone, and I made myself seem like a thirsty disaster, and I just made the worst impression."

Okay, two things: 1) You probably didn't, and 2) nobody cares.

"Stop trying to plug your book."

This book? Called *Nobody Cares?* Thank you for buying it. (It also makes a great gift!) I read a piece recently about how nobody really thinks about what somebody else has done — unless it's fucking egregious — beyond seven seconds or so. So trust that everyone is so caught up in their own shit that they haven't for one minute thought about yours.

"No, but I saw one person give another a look."

Okay then, fine. They gave each other a look. About you. And? Do you really give a fuck? Who are these people, anyway? They were upset that you spoke loudly or said something inoffensively unfunny? To them? Okay. Sure. Also: not every person is going to represent Your People, so take it in stride that you will likely never see these fools again. And if you do, you're not enemies, you're just going to stick to conversations about the weather.

"But what if they talk about me?"

They probably will. But I mean, hi: we all talk shit. If you think I'm going to sit here and pretend I love every person and do not actively engage in conversations about why so-and-so's tone cemented our eternal feud and animosity, you are about to be very disappointed. I'm a human, and so are 99.9% of other people. We don't like everybody, and we talk shit sometimes. Tale as old as time.

"Okay, so I should just take shit from people?"

Here's the thing: no. But also, it's a control thing, right? We want to control the way we're seen. We want to be in charge of the way we're received. Even though that's impossible. Try as we might (and believe me, I've tried), there's nothing we can do to sway certain minds. LET IT GO. REVEL IN THE SWEET LIFE YOU HAVE.

"So, I should just stop caring about what everyone thinks of me."

I mean, yes. Kind of? Yes. Well . . . no, yes. Care about what your family thinks, or your close friends, or if your employer is like "I love how much you're into hats, but you really have to stop wearing the falafel hat from *She's All That* because this is a law firm, and you're in the middle of a custody battle," then take off the fucking hat. But everybody else? No thank you.

"Okay —"

Here's the thing. Deep down, we know if we're good people or not. Right? Like, when you fuck up, you *know* you've fucked up. And there's a difference between "I've been calling her Crandall!" (one of my favorite *Simpsons* lines) and "I have just said and done something terrible that requires immediate attention." YOU KNOW. So, did you come away from your weird, embarrassing whatever-the-fuck convinced that you are a bad person?

"No."

Obviously not. Also, if you're that consumed about a five-second-or-whatever interaction, odds are you're very careful not to be a piece of shit. So, you said a thing that got a look, or you spoke too loudly, and now you've just identified a person who'll probably not end up being a wonderful friend.

"That's it?"

Dude, that's IT. And while we all love to shit-talk amongst our nearest and dearest, I'm willing to assume that no one is genuinely consumed by a person to the point of talking ONLY about that person. Like, it's weird if someone is obsessed with the way you pronounced "pear" at a party. It's weird if an entire dinner is about what was wrong with your outfit. That's weird for *them*, not you.

And also, here's the other thing about not always being universally loved: NO ONE IS. Not a single soul. Some people hate Beyoncé. Some people hate Harry Styles. Some people hate Rihanna. Those people are idiots, and I hate them, but that's the truth. And if not even the Holy Trinity are universally loved, what hope is there for the rest of us? So you might as well just be and do you. When I find out someone doesn't like me, after writing them off as a balloon animal who isn't worthy of my time, I just think WELL, TOO BAD FOR THEM, I GUESS. And, like Arya Stark (that's her name, right?), add them to the list of people I will mention when I win the first of many awards to remind them: fuck you.

"Wait, but you said that nobody cares and to revel in your sweet life, and —"

Listen, man, I may believe those things and subscribe to them, but part of my sweet life includes pettiness. In the immortal words of my friend Sarah, "I don't forget."

"You're frightening me."

And therefore you are giving me the respect I deserve.

"Get out of my house, Anne T. Donahue."

Anne T. Donahue? WHY, SHE'S BEEN DEAD FOR 35 YEARS!

"I'm serious."

Yeah, I'm so sorry. I'm absolutely going to overthink this, actually.

FRIENDSHIP MISTAKES I HAVE MADE
(SO YOU DON'T HAVE TO)

Like most of us, I often assume that I am perfect. I tell myself I am the greatest friend in the world, that I have never done anything wrong, and that any person who interacts with me is blessed and lucky and being smiled down upon by whatever higher power they believe in.

And then, after a few moments of beautiful delusion, I convince myself that my friends will all soon realize that I'm not as great as they thought I was, and my next birthday party will consist of them telling me why we'll never speak again. (This is why I'll never have a birthday party.) Which isn't a totally unfounded fear. While I know even the best and longest friendships have peaks and valleys, I have lived that valley life hard.

My long journeys to the bottom would justify "accidentally" deleting this chapter in lieu of trying to put a positive spin on all the friendship lessons I've learned, bless us, every one.

But alas. Lessons are learned by acknowledging the grossest and cruelest parts of ourselves, so to spare your best friend tears on their birthday, or them wondering why you ghosted for three years without explanation, I present you with the mistakes I've made so you don't have to. Because if I've learned anything, it's that you should do what I say — definitely not what I do.

MISTAKE #1: PROJECTING YOUR INSECURITIES ONTO YOUR FRIEND (AT THE MALL ON HER BIRTHDAY)

My friend Judith and I have a long-standing joke: when it's one of our birthdays, the other suggests that in celebration of another year lived, we should go to the mall and yell at each other. Because I did this to her in the spring of 2012.

At the time, I was a sad person. I was a self-medicating alcoholic, two-time dropout who was tens of thousands of dollars in debt, and Judith was a woman seemingly sailing through her undergrad and, despite being four years younger than me, she was (and is) one of the most grounded and balanced people I knew. In short, how dare she.

We went to the mall on her birthday because both of us love the mall. We'd gone for breakfast before and planned a day of snacking and shopping. But as we were rifling through the underwear table at American Eagle, she told me about her plans to move to the area of Toronto I held responsible for my disaster life, and I casually responded, "I hate hipsters."

Judith looked confused and said that wasn't really fair; that many of her best friends would be categorized as hipsters, and sweeping generalizations don't tend to be helpful. Furious she couldn't understand that it was everybody else's fault my life had hit bottom (likely because she had no idea I was *at* bottom), I kept going. I said that I hated the type of lifestyle she and her friends had, that I hated the city she was moving to, that I was better and more mature and everybody should know it. In the years since, Judith has told me that once you realize you're in an argument with me, it's too late and you've already lost (regardless of whether I'm right or wrong), but in 2012, she'd never seen this side of me before. She stood there, on her birthday, trying to figure out what I was actually angry about, and when she wouldn't let me just drop it, I began twisting her questions into accusations and left her standing there with tears in her eyes. "I told you I didn't want to talk about this anymore," I said. "I wish you could've respected that."

The rest of the day was quiet and awkward, but we still got snacks, and I apologized for "seeming angry" before going home and writing her a lengthy Facebook message reiterating how disrespected I felt by her not letting me just drop an argument I'd started for no reason in front of many lacy boybriefs. And then, despite her asking me to hang out and catch up, I avoided her for *months* until she had a housewarming dinner I felt I couldn't get out of.

Judith treats her friends like family, so her capacity for forgiveness is more generous than mine. (I treat my friends like mafia family — which means I will do anything for them unless they hurt me, and then I will order their deaths.) (Just kidding.) (Or am I?) And while I apologized for "being so weird" that spring and summer, it wasn't until I began delving deeper into my mental and emotional shit that I came up to acknowledge how much I'd projected onto her. It wasn't her fault that I felt bananas or that I had to live with my parents. It wasn't her fault that she was excelling at school and I couldn't seem to land regular work. It wasn't her fault that she had a boyfriend who loved her while I kept pursuing various incarnations of David Blaine.

So remember *that* before you start yelling at your friend in front of an underwear table. At least have the decency to yell at them in the food court, where mall arguments belong.

MISTAKE #2: NOT TELLING YOUR FRIEND ABOUT YOUR INTENTION TO HOOK UP WITH HER EX

In grade 11, my official crush was on Chad. But I was soon distracted by his friend Ben, who I decided would be the Harry to my Sally. We'd been fast food coworkers, pals who talked regularly on ICQ and hung out platonically — but he was dating Alana, who I had yet to become friends with. Ben, according to me (and only to me — definitely never to him), was my *best* friend. And that meant we would end up together.

Obviously, I didn't relay any of this to anyone during the course of Ben and Alana's twoish-month relationship. I'd been jealous to start, but after befriending Alana one night over cigarettes and mutual anxieties, we'd become friends in our own right, and her boyfriend was an afterthought instead of one at the forefront. Until they broke up.

Here's a red flag, kids: anyone who asks you to keep your relationship a complete secret is probably not worth your time. (Unless he's royalty. And even then, that might not be a shitshow you want to wade into.) In Ben's opinion, I wasn't just Alana's best friend, and therefore off-limits publicly, but a social misstep who put his Cool Guy clout at risk. Thus, our hookups could happen only under the umbrella of discretion and after solemn promises (from me) that no one would ever find out, so he wouldn't be judged by his friends. And I, desperate to make him realize how special I was, agreed. Kind of. I told all my friends who *weren't* Alana and pushed her to date a friend of ours who seemed interested so I could ease my conscience. Don't do that.

The good news is that it worked out — for everyone but me. Alana dated her boyfriend for a handful of years, and he turned out to be kind, cool, and all you could ask for in a teen boyfriend. And me? I ended things with Ben after he called the girl he wanted to date literally minutes after we'd fooled around. I sent him an email saying I didn't think it was working out, and he sent one back saying he agreed and planned to ask out the girl he'd called after we hooked up, anyway. Cool!

A few months later, I finally fessed up to Alana as I'd become consumed by guilt. I'd been so calculating in orchestrating my Ben situation that I hadn't even bothered to see if the boyfriend I'd urged her into dating was actually worth her time.

"I hooked up with Ben!" I confessed one night while we were roaming the neighborhood.

"Oh!" she said. "Good for you! Recently?"

And I laid it all out for her: the sneaking around, the lies, the deceit, the fact he was now dating a girl he'd once brought over for pancakes (because I was naïve enough to think that if I earned her adulation, she'd be the Carrie Fisher to my Meg Ryan and suggest he and I date each other). I told her about the email he'd sent me one night after I kissed him goodbye before walking into my house: "By the way," he'd written. "Don't do that again. This is not what this is — I don't want you to think we're dating." Definitely not the Harry to my Sally.

Alana laughed between dutiful "What a dick!" responses. "By the way, I wouldn't have been mad!" she said. "You should've just told me!"

MISTAKE #3: ABANDONING SHIP

In too many ways, I am Don Draper. I'm smart, I'm confident-sounding, I could be played by Jon Hamm, I look terrific in slacks, and I'm brilliant at ghosting on situations that have the capacity to get messy. With age, I've learned that abandoning ship will only make everything worse, but for no less than 29 years, I assumed my unexplained absence was a viable and legitimate way to handle conflict. Some memorable episodes:

Problem: My friends were angry at me for bailing on
    birthdays or long-standing plans without any real
    explanation.
Healthy solution: I would have to be vulnerable
    and elaborate on the social anxiety I had yet to

feel comfortable with on my own terms while
simultaneously shattering the belief that I was
flawless and/or godlike.

My solution: Bail until I wasn't invited to anything
anymore.

Problem: I decided that a friend and I had grown apart
because they didn't like the same bands as I did,
so instead of trying to find common ground or
accepting that people are different, I stopped talking
to them.

Healthy solution: I would have to make peace with
the inevitable realization that independence is an
important part of friendship.

My solution: Silently force that independence on them
by refusing to commit to plans in any capacity for the
entirety of time.

Problem: I cut off wise, old friends in lieu of new friends
who enabled me because I was only telling those new
friends part of my story (and of my capacity for self-
destruction).

Healthy solution: I would have to acknowledge and
admit that I had many problems, friendship being the
least pressing one.

My solution: Please see the essay on alcoholism.

Problem: I interpreted texts as something passive-
aggressive or judgmental, and instead of saying,

"What does that mean?" I'd just ignore all texts until we finally came face-to-face at a Christmas party years later and were forced to confront the palpable tension.

Healthy solution: I would have to risk confronting what that meant.

My solution: Bring on the Ghost of Christmas Past.

So just tell your friends the truth. Tell them you're angry, sad, annoyed, hurt, tired, anxious; that you'd rather eat poison than go to a birthday party at a fucking nightclub again, and that you'll just take them out for dinner instead.

Save ghosting for when you're an actual denizen of the underworld and can appear silently in the bathroom mirror of your worst enemy, standing behind them as you scar them for life.

MISTAKE #4: MAKING IT ABOUT YOU

When working retail in my early twenties, a friend of mine got a phone call at work letting her know that a close friend of hers was in the ICU. The event was tragic and unexpected, and it hit her hard. As a result, I was asked to come in and close for her that night. I didn't want to. I was in a pair of faded PJ pants and a T-shirt with seagulls on it, and I was watching *Forensic Files* and pretty sure I was getting a cold. I went in wearing exactly what I'd been solving crime in and complained to customers and staff alike about how hard done by I was to do her this favor.

I opened the back door to the breakroom and found her crying.

"He's still in the hospital, right?" I said, stone-faced, before offering a hug or any means of comfort.

"Yeah —"

"Well, he might not die," I said matter-of-factly. "So don't overreact."

I put my coat and bag in my locker and complained about how tired I was and how I hoped I wouldn't get everybody sick since it was obvious I was also at death's door. She kept crying, and I kept reminding her that until her friend was pronounced dead, "you never know, so calm down." She left soon after, and he passed away shortly after that.

My friend has a capacity for love and forgiveness and compassion and empathy that I don't think I ever will. She is kindness and generosity personified. She is the type of friend who manages to dole out real and concrete advice while exposing her own vulnerabilities to make you feel more comfortable. She hugs like no one I've ever met. And she never brought up what I'd said to her. I finally apologized for it.

"Oh, Annie!" she said. "It's okay. I know you were frustrated that you had to come in."

Which, like, no. Nobody cares about your bullshit when there's an actual tragedy or a life on the line. Shut up, stop speaking, and don't make it about you. Most things — 99% of things — are not about you, and when another person is combating trauma, they're especially not.

And for the record, I did get a terrible cold. And I deserved it.

MISTAKE #5: TOO MUCH HONESTY

In 2006, I wanted to look "indie" and "hip," so I dyed my brown hair blond and cut it into a shag-mullet. And, despite looking terrible and the worst, I was not judged. My friends promised that my chicken-fat-yellow hair looked great, that I would easily be mistaken for the lead singer in a cool band. I just had to get used to it.

In 1989, I wasn't as accepting.

My friend and next-door neighbor had long, beautiful blond hair. She had natural curls in a way I never would, and I was understandably in awe. Which meant that when she cut it all off into a mullet, she'd shattered not just her mother's dreams, but mine too. I was horrified. I was disgusted. I was appalled that she didn't see her grave mistake in taking the kitchen scissors and mutilating something I couldn't have.

I ignored her for days, turning down her invitations for playdates and telling her I didn't want to play outside with anyone — only to play with the other neighbors minutes later. Finally, she offered a bribe. She stood at my front door with two freezies, one blue and one white — my favorite colors.

"Annie," she said, handing one to me, "do you wanna come outside and play?"

I took the freezie and looked at her. I smiled softly, looking upon her and her bad hair in pity. "No thank you," I said, closing the door.

I wandered into the kitchen, where my aunt and mom were sitting. They asked where I'd gotten the freezie.

"Julia gave it to me so I would play with her, but I said no."

I have never found myself so quickly whisked outside and into the company of a person I didn't want to be around. I barely felt my mother's hands on my shoulders as she guided me out the front door, ordering me to play with my friend for a least an hour because I was being rude. What was rude, I remember thinking, was cutting one's hair into such a terrible shape.

I patted my own mushroom cut and reveled in my excellent taste. Perfection was a curse, and clearly I was suffering from it.

BUT, FOR THE RECORD: I AM NOT FUN

It's important that you know, dear reader, that I am not fun. If we have hung out and you had fun, odds are that you're not fun either. I like sitting, eating beige food, driving around, walking around malls, buying stuff at malls, and taking a lot of photos for Instagram. And I hate everything else. I hate most parties, and I hate clubs, and I hate bars that don't have chairs, and the only concerts I care about involve Harry Styles, Beyoncé, and assigned seating — but not if they start any later than 10 p.m.

I know I used to be fun. I used to go out dancing and to concerts and suggest that my friends and I "make an appearance" at parties. I used to exclaim things like "I'm down for whatever!" and sleep on the floor of friends' houses and say I didn't care where we went for dinner. I went to DJ nights. I suffered frequently from FOMO. I used words like "adventure" and "exciting" together in a sentence, but not in the form "It is exciting that we managed to avoid an adventure," as I do today.

With age, I've come to embrace who I am. In my case, I am a person with a fantastic capacity for setting boundaries. More than I love saying yes, I love saying no. I love rescheduling. I love cancelling and being cancelled on. I take delight in declining Facebook event invitations. I love going to an uncool family chain restaurant with a best friend and talking shit for three hours, blissfully aware we will see nobody we know. I love not knowing what cool bands are playing at a music festival I don't care about and will never go to. Ultimately, I love not doing shit I hate. Freedom.

But it took me a long time to get here. If we're being specific, it took about 31 years and was crystallized by personal realizations, like that to successfully be a living person, you have to cut something out. For me — and the majority of my close friends — that was agreeing to do things that made me miserable.

Nothing in this world bonds people together like collectively hating a thing that everybody else seems to love. The majority of my adult friendships formed over the realization that we dislike the same people or the same scene or the same trend, and the rest have been forged through detesting everything else. So in the celebration of freedom through disdain, here is a starter list of things I hate. Feel free to hate them too.

Especially brunch.

BRUNCH

Fuck brunch. Fuck it. I will not wait in line for eggs and salmon when I can make eggs in my home and defrost smoked salmon in my sink. I will not pay $10 for a plate of leaves. I will not pretend that I am happy sitting alongside a 14-top table, propped up against a stranger whose hangover is overpowering the scent of my $25 breakfast. I do not think it's "cute" that it costs extra for sparkling water, nor do I want my pancakes to be seasonal or rich in flaxseed.

I am not interested in brunch. Brunch is not interested in me. When all-day fast food breakfast was introduced to the masses, I knew the rest of the world was on my side.

SOMMELIERS

I am not impressed by how much you know about wine. I also know a lot about wine, and that's because I consumed it in great quantities, often without a glass, alone. No one's identity should be defined by how much they know about grapes, nor should anyone be shamed for how little they know about them. If you want to earn my respect via alcohol, be the ghost of my Irish great-grandmother, who bootlegged in Canada to ensure my grandpa and his siblings survived. And honestly, something tells me that Esther Watson Donahue wouldn't suffer sommeliers either.

ANY CONCERT WITHOUT CHAIRS

As I've mentioned, I refuse. I understand that this isn't a particular band's fault, but know that if your band is playing a chairless venue, I will not be there. I need to sit down and put my shit down on the floor in front of me. Plus, I would like to enjoy a beverage and a snack, using my lap as a kind of buffet stand. Standing in the corner of a hot venue feeling a twenty-something named Reid sweat his mustache on me does not allow for either of the aforementioned.

When I was 24 and 25, I went to concerts almost every night, and I wore out my patience for concert attendees back then. Now, even when leaving a concert with assigned seats, I channel Billy Zane in *Titanic*, grabbing the hand of whatever friend I'm with and yelling, "I have a child!" in an attempt to escape quickly.

DJ NIGHTS
Can you even fucking imagine?

THE BEACH
The beach is a trap. It is a villain and a bore. I grew up going to the beach with my parents, more psyched for the drive up north than I ever was to sit around watching waves. And then, as a teen, the beach was where you'd see and be seen; where, after over an hour spent driving to a Great Lake, you'd descend on the sand and pray that the guy you liked would be there (and that he hadn't gone to one of the other beaches situated an equal distance away). One year, a bunch of us went to Grand Bend for Canada Day, and all the boys we went to school with got nipple piercings at the same time. I should've known then that I didn't belong. Also, I got a heat rash.

There are always too many people at the beach. A woman I'd never met once infringed on my towel territory by kind of sitting on it. Another year, a bird shit on my leg. Too crowded. Too hot. Too boring. Too sandy.

I went to two beaches in 2016, and both times I spent maybe half an hour onshore before putting my feet in the water and congratulating myself for engaging with nature, and then I decided which restaurant to go to following my escape from the beach. I also pulled my calves because my body wasn't built for walking on sand. I am not Luke Skywalker. This is not Tatooine.

CHEESE

I hate cheese. I hate cheese as a lactose-intolerant person in a largely lactose-tolerant world, and I hate cheese as a person offended by the smell of cheese. I hated it as a child, I hated it as a teen. I do not miss cheese on my pizza, because it tasted like elastics.

Also: I do not want to try your almond cheese or your soft cheese or your soy cheese. I would rather eat socks.

THE VIP MYTH

None of us are important, and all of us are the worst. You know this, and I know this, but anyone thirsting for VIP status and sections does not know this. And as a result, we all must suffer.

We all must wait in a line created solely to make a restaurant or bar look popular. We all must pretend to care about a velvet rope and whoever happens to be behind it. We're left to assume that someone's seats are automatically better than ours, or that every movie star is just out of sight in that sectioned-off room reserved for anybody with a certain number of Instagram followers.

But here's what I've learned after spending time in maybe four VIP areas in the history of my time on this planet: they make me want to die. They are not special. I am not special because I am in them. The VIP section is just an area with free snacks (maybe) and a security dude who did not see his night playing out like this. The best VIP section is always your or your friend's car with the *Hamilton* soundtrack playing as you eat McDonald's.

MUSIC FESTIVALS/FILM FESTIVALS/MOST FESTIVALS

I cared so much once. I lived for music festivals and for action and for glory and for celebrity-sighting at the Toronto International Film Festival. I lived for the sad belief that I really belonged. But I sure wanted everybody who saw me to know that I had been chosen as an employee or a journalist or a person important enough to own a lanyard — which is why I wore mine miles away from venues, just waiting for people to ask if I was famous. They didn't.

And then I just stopped caring. I didn't have room to care about who was at what anymore.

Which isn't to say anybody who does care is making the wrong choice. I was never in it for the right reasons: I wanted to feel special and cool and was in no way an active participant in culture or any definitive scene. I felt out of place at industry parties, backstage at festivals, and especially while trying to act super-chill in the bathroom with Kate Winslet as she and her team changed her outfit. My TIFF will never again be as magical as the one where I interrupted a strange man trying to pawn his mixtape off onto Rachel McAdams. I did it by loudly bringing up a guy I heard she knew from high school. And I know firsthand she's an excellent actress because she did a very convincing job of making it seem like I was being a completely normal person at a TIFF party.

No more.

GAME OF THRONES

For years I told people it was "on my list." For years I said that I'll binge it when I have the flu. But no: *Game of Thrones* has never been on my list, and I will never binge it under any circumstances (especially if I have the flu).

I have never watched *Game of Thrones* and I will never watch *Game of Thrones*. It's my dragon-filled version of *The Wire*: I know it's good, I know everybody likes it, but too much time has passed, and I will never watch it because I never wanted to in the first place, and I have been lying about intending to since I was an infant.

RUFFLES

Ruffles are a brand of potato chip in Canada and also an international fashion trend, and I hope you know me well enough by now to know that I would never use precious pulp and paper to condemn a snack food.

However, the fashion trend can burn in hell. It is impossible to look intimidating in a ruffled shirt. It is impossible to stomp across the street and yell menacingly about something in a ruffled dress unless you are Beyoncé in the "Hold Up" video. No part of me was built to wear ruffles. Therefore, I hate them.

CAMPING

I have never been camping. (I have slept with the windows open in my room, and in the backseat of a friend's Jeep while drunk at a bush party. Does that count? No? Who cares.) Even as a small child, I knew that luxuries like beds and walls and locked doors and an indoor flushing toilet were important to me.

My parents don't camp, my grandparents didn't camp, and I am proud to continue the tradition of wondering what the fuck is wrong with you if you'd rather "rough it" than spend time indoors, you nature-loving freak. Why are you choosing to shit on the land?

EATING ON PATIOS AT NIGHT

I love eating outside — until you leave after eating your cold-after-two-minutes meal covered in so many mosquito bites that you can't sleep for two full nights so you stay up Googling West Nile Virus symptoms.

THE HIERARCHY OF HIP

I say "absolutely not" out loud regularly to the majority of Facebook invites and have actively fought the urge to comment "WOW WE GET IT" on any Instagram photo where it seems like the person is pretending not to know their photo was being taken — by themselves, in a bathroom — and then subsequently posted on social media.

I don't want to go to "cool" parties. When someone uses Twitter to elevate themselves over pop culture, I want to scream. (Fun fact: hating *Hamilton* does not make you interesting.) My favorite clothes are the ones I like and feel powerful in, and I would rather bathe a cat than pretend to have anything other than my usually mainstream taste. I actively cut off people who believe their taste in movies or music or TV shows makes them complex or multidimensional. Nobody cares if you don't like Drake.

When I was a kid, my Uncle Dan taught me his motto — "I got no time" — but it took me well into my adult years to begin applying it to myself. Because I don't. And you don't. Hanging one's identity on coolness, hipness, or cultural elitism is as ludicrous as calling yourself a lumber-jack because you wore plaid once. That's not how anything works.

As a grown-ass woman, I think people who work hard are cool. I think someone who gives a shit about other people is rad. I think being able to hang out with a friend you trust and genuinely like and eat a ton of junk food with while actively avoiding a gallery opening for an acquaintance you don't like is a dream. I think the mall is the best.

The thing is, you can't know peace until you decide that you're not going to do the shit you hate anymore. You can't know joy or freedom until you ignore an event invite and instead opt to microwave a hot dog you're going to eat over the sink.

Bliss is boundaries. It is the admission of dislike, and the embrace of limitations and flaws. To me, my life looks better for saying hell no.

So no, I'm not fun if your definition of fun is doing any of the aforementioned. But I'll tell you what always *will* be a good time: telling you guys all about it, so that you will never again invite me to a music festival you have to camp at.

THE LEAST
INTERESTING THING

I spent a long time trying to be interesting. I wanted to be complicated, I wanted to have "overcome" an obstacle that made me seem brave and worth listening to. In high school, I over-romanticized *Girl, Interrupted* and longed to be as complex as Winona Ryder's or Angelina Jolie's characters (so I dutifully typed their monologues into my ICQ away messages and awaited questions about my well-being to roll in). In my early twenties, I gauged my worth with Facebook shares and Twitter likes: to rack up a shit-ton of either meant that I was special and deep and innately profound. My sensationalized self-realizations magnified by digital platforms would help me finally feel special in some capacity (or at least up my follower count). While some people were very good at articulating their mental health realities on the internet, I was . . . not.

Not that I cared. By 25, I was so desperate for discerning qualities that I'd bring up anything even remotely "wrong." I pitched a memoir about my brush with disordered eating as a teen: I'd spent most of my younger years yo-yoing between sizes oo and 10, but got too scared when I finally lost my period to keep starving myself. (The pitch was politely declined because that was basically the entire story.) I'd revel in how I'd spent most of my life chasing not-so-nice guys as if I was the only one in the world who had. Having semi-noted my addictive personality, I toyed with officially announcing that I had a Drinking Problem, but dismissed the notion when I realized that going public with that would mean I'd have to stop drinking. (I was a few years out from being ready for that.)

I wanted to be complicated, and my vanilla life wasn't giving me any material. Instead, it felt like a blueprint in bad decision-making cradled by the safety of family and friends: no matter how much I failed, I still knew I had someplace to stay and a support system of pals ready and willing to meet me for drinks. Real creatives struggled. They suffered. They walked that long, hard road by themselves. What every other person would see as privilege, I saw as tragic, the reason my life lacked intrigue.

But I began to see the similarities between my dad and me as an extension of that. He articulated his worries about my largely pro bono writing career by raising his voice during conversations about my finances. I responded with mean one-liners instead of explaining how I planned to eventually make a living. On our best days, both of us are loud, quick to flare, and prone to mask genuine concern by getting angry. So, one morning after a particularly cutting back-and-forth, I woke up and decided to move. I'd use a recently approved line of credit to pay my $800/month rent, since I only earned about $200. I fueled my irrationality with the belief that my dad and mom didn't "get" me.

After my dad left for work the next morning, I loudly explained to my mom how important it was that I "escape" our family home, brushing off her concerns about how I'd survive when the line of credit maxed out, or how I'd pay off my maxed-out Visa. Which only frustrated me more. She didn't understand that I was an artist; that to live in an authentic way, I'd need to be free of their kindness and worries and repeated reminders that writing essays for $10 wasn't going to provide enough to live on. They didn't get that I was doing precious, important, and extraordinary work. They didn't see what I was capable of. So, fuck them.

High on mania-lite, I put out a call for an apartment on Twitter, booked a viewing that night, and landed my first grown-up apartment within about 12 hours, reinforcing the belief I had in myself and my potential. Everybody was wrong but me: I was a genius who had the guts to go after what I wanted, and anyone who dared challenge me was clearly out to see me fail. I held on to this feeling for days, lording it over my dad and mom, and using it as "look who's successful *now*" currency at Christmas. In February 2011, I moved out of my parents' house in Cambridge and into an apartment in Toronto that I couldn't afford.

I spent the first half of my downtown life trying to resurrect the same conviction I'd had in December. Now forced to confront my financial reality, I accepted any and all work I could get before days of rationality would give way to high-highs and paralyzing lows. One afternoon, I paid a Visa bill using rolled coins before spending the last of my credit line on a candle I believed would change my life. (It did not.) Another day, I up and decided it was time to stop working as a music journalist — my destiny now lay in writing TV. (Something I'd never tried before.) Sometimes, I'd stay in bed until I forced myself up, sluggishly making my way to the kitchen where I'd make the first of many pots of coffee, unable to do anything until well into the evening, when a few glasses of wine would convince me I could write again.

I wrote lists and comedy pieces for free and abandoned most of my existing editors, which meant that just shy of a year after moving downtown, I was finally living the dream of earning approximately $250/month (maybe). But, determined to eclipse my financial reality with my oft-manic persona, I leaned into my overconfidence and self-importance and descended on my hometown for the holidays, acting high and mighty and treating everyone I saw like garbage if I felt they'd never acknowledged how awesome I was.

I embarked on a quest to make everybody I'd ever met aware that I'd "made it"; that I'd fled our old stomping grounds and graduated to greatness, unlike those who still lived and worked and existed within walking distance of our high school. They didn't need know about my diet of macaroni and butter (sauce is expensive), or the fact that I'd recently Googled "dinner recipes for stale bread." They'd see exactly what I demanded they see: a mysterious, interesting, and beautifully complicated young woman who'd live to see them rue the day they counted her out. (Which was never actually a thing they'd done — but that's the power of self-mythologizing.) I was Anne T. Donahue, a writer who was forced to use a middle initial to prevent being mistaken for the creator of *CSI*, who had absolutely nothing going terribly wrong in her life, who had it all figured out. And there was nothing like making everybody feel terrible about themselves by calling their lives "cute" to help hide the fact that mine was a lie.

And that's when the emotional gong show truly began. When I got back to Toronto a few days later, I realized the holidays had delayed the mail and, with it, my paychecks. Which meant that I couldn't afford January's rent and was officially fucked: my line of credit was tapped out, my Visa was maxed, and any rolled coins I'd managed to save had gone towards Christmas gifts I'd insisted on buying (for myself). I called my parents and begged them for rent money, using the one-time-only lifeline loan they'd offered me when I'd left home. I swore to pay them back as soon as I could. They agreed to send the money, but they used my moment of vulnerability to stage a surprise attack: why not just move home and save? Why not pay down what I'd racked up, then move back out when I could afford to turn on my heat?

Because I'd rather die, I reminded them. How dare they attempt to coerce me into moving backwards. Hadn't my living downtown proven to them how successful I was, how capable of independence? I shut down their suggestion by promising that they'd get every penny of their loan back in weeks, and that this was just a little blip on my flawless financial history — a mistake at the hands of the postal service — and I wished they'd recognize that. I couldn't believe they failed to see that I was making good money on a reliable schedule and it was fine. (TOTALLY FINE!!!)

Interest payments and phone and electricity bills had made my living situation impossible. Even if my checks all came at once and were for hundreds more than I had invoiced, I'd still only have about $20 to last until February. I'd already sold all my records to spring for a few cans of Chef Boyardee, and my license had been suspended for unpaid parking tickets. Still, I maintained my delusional narrative. When I got sick with the flu, it wasn't because I hadn't seen a fresh vegetable in weeks (popcorn is a vegetable!), but because I was just one of those people who got sick a lot.

I called home a few days after my rent request to ask my mom what I should do to avoid dying from what I assumed to be tuberculosis. And at some point between cough syrup recommendations and reminders to rest up and watch *Mary Tyler Moore*, she gently suggested I move back home. Again.

"You can't afford to live there, sweetie."

"But I'm fine!" I said between coughing fits. I rushed to find proof of why I should continue to live the way I had been. I looked out my window at the brick wall of the adjacent Victorian home. "I'll never be able to find an apartment this great again!"

My apartment was a glorified bachelor on the second floor of a very old house. It was what could be called cozy, but with paper-thin walls and mice and several colonies of spiders I'd begun killing with a Swiffer broom wrapped in paper towel. I could hear the guy who lived above me pee or roll around in his bed, and I prayed every night that he would never have a sex guest because his bed was right above my own. Which is all to say, thousands of people have found and lived in apartments like mine. You might even be living in one right now. This apartment was not Meg Ryan's in *You've Got Mail* (the Taj Mahal of apartments), but the most ordinary apartment in the world.

My mom sat quietly on the other end of the call, and then said that my childhood room would be waiting if I wanted it. I loudly objected as I began reenacting Fantine's death scene from *Les Misérables*.

The thing about stress is that it will kill you. Most of us know this because we're human adults with a basic understanding of how health works. But during the winter of 2012, I believed that I was immune to stress; that whatever was happening to me was some kind of endurance test that I'd obviously ace — despite having no real plan or income or access to vitamins. Within a week of recovering from my first flu, I got hit with another one. Feeling sorry for myself, I caved and went home for soup and sustenance and hangs with my cat, and when I started to feel better, I transplanted myself to a local Starbucks to see my best friend, Erica.

I've known Erica since we were seven. We bonded over *Practical Magic* (Jimmy Angelov is as hot as he is problematic), and we've fought over me acting like a dick (a running theme for much of our teen years). When Erica sat down and told me she wanted to move to the country, I knew I could be honest with her, and with myself. I told her that I needed to move home. And, in typical Erica fashion, she congratulated me on my overdue revelation and told me she was psyched that we'd get to live so close to each other again. No harm, no foul, no shame. I sat beaming like an idiot because it felt like I could breathe for the first time in a long time. And just like that, I had it all figured out again.

Unlike the me of mere days ago who'd sat drinking warm wine in her cold apartment, I had evolved into a self-aware woman of action. I came home, announced my new life plan to my parents, and immediately began thinking about all the things I could buy with the money I normally would've spent on rent. Debt payments didn't matter; the Visa people would understand. I'd never be sad again, and I would always feel exactly as powerful as I felt in the moment of my big revelation. I was the living incarnation of Mary Tyler Moore tossing her beret in the air.

My landlords, Vinnie and Reggie, were a very sweet elderly Italian couple who didn't communicate in English very well, but took an active interest in their tenants' lives when they were weren't screaming at their grandchildren or strange adult son. They asked me regularly if I had a boyfriend, or why I didn't live with my parents, so I figured my plans to vacate would bring us all merriment, or at least some closure. Vinnie sweetly said that a girl like me belonged with her parents, wished me the best, and confirmed I'd be gone by the end of the month.

In the wake of this clean, mature, and newfound closure, I felt zero merriment. Nothing like Mary Tyler Moore. I emotionally crashed and shattered my brain.

I went upstairs, sat on my bed, and looked around the apartment I'd made a home despite knowing I had no real business having one of my own. I thought about how I'd once felt so grown-up here. Just a few weeks earlier, my friends had come over to celebrate my first anniversary of downtown living, and I'd been so proud. I looked out my windows at my stunning view of the bricks and my neighbor's living room and realized I would never see sights like this ever again. I thought about losing my independent space to share with my parents, who cared about me, in a neighborhood I knew way too well — how gross familiarity was. I thought about how much money I didn't have and how I was a failure and a hack and a fraud, and, and, and. How sick I was, how tired, how helpless. I opened a bottle of wine and drank from it and started to cry, and I didn't stop until the wine and the Gravol and the cold medicine put me to sleep. It felt like something had broken, and I couldn't put my finger on what. It was the worst feeling I've ever had, and even talking about it almost a decade later makes me feel sad and terrible.

On a bright morning the following October, I sat in my doctor's office, waiting for him to bring me a mental health questionnaire. Two nights earlier, I'd finally told my mom I thought something was wrong because I couldn't control my moods. Since moving home (under the cloak of darkness — I was so embarrassed to leave Toronto that I drove my stuff home in my car over several nights), I'd become too sad, too low, and too ready to cry when I wasn't busy being too ready to yell. Or I was too up, too happy, too excitable, too much. I'd believe I could conquer the world (like a dictator, not like Elle Woods) but then have to drink myself to sleep to get out of the nightmare in my head. I flip-flopped between cripplingly anxious and recklessly self-destructive, and I'd only gotten deeper in debt. I had no self-control — from how much alcohol I drank to how much money I spent. I split my time being convinced I was either the worst writer or the best one, and while I might have a day or two of reprieve or balance, the highs and lows began striking more frequently and with more drama than an episode of *The Bachelor*. In a word: woof.

I'd been an emotional kid, but the older I got, the more outsized my feelings became. At 21, I once got so incensed about my parents' plans to repaint the house that I burst into angry tears and counted the pictures hanging on the walls in an attempt to prove how much they were inconveniencing me. (There were seven pictures in the room we were in, and I will never not laugh at the memory of screaming "SEVEN PICTURES!" as though it were a viable point.)

A couple of months later, I had to pull the car over because I was berating my mom for losing a map to the point that I was crying so hard I couldn't see. The next summer, I spent most evenings in tears at the cash registers of my retail job, convinced I'd never escape the industry or get rid of the stress-induced IBS I'd given myself. But 2012 was next level.

Before talking to my mom about how out of control I felt, I'd spent the night crying alone in the park I grew up going to, chain smoking, because the guy that I liked hadn't texted me back. And even amidst my tears and Camels and repeated utterings of "I'm going to die alone," I knew I was acting out of my mind. I knew I looked fucking crazy. I knew if the guy could see me reacting this way, he'd block my number. But I still couldn't stop, and that's what scared me.

My emotions had become all-encompassing. Like the night I'd given my landlord notice, I couldn't see or feel anything other than the most extreme version of the worst-case scenario. Because here's the thing: in those polarizing moments of ups or downs, what you're feeling in that moment can't be reasoned with or told to slow down, let alone stop. I looked across the park at the swings my friends and I used to hang out on and wondered what the fuck was wrong with me. Why couldn't I feel the way I used to, once upon a time? I wanted to feel invincible the way I sometimes did — or better yet, I wanted no feeling at all.

So there I sat in my doctor's office, filling out that questionnaire. He was kind and thorough and made sure not to jump to conclusions. He asked if anybody in my family was or had been bipolar, and when I told him about my great aunt, he nodded understandingly. I told him I knew that how I was feeling wasn't normal, and I joked about relating too much to Carrie from *Homeland*. He sympathetically smiled the way a lot of people do when I make jokes about bipolar disorder now.

I'm lucky because my doctor is one of the friendliest and most genuine people I know. He told me he'd like to start me on a low dose of lithium and very slowly work our way up until my body was at a treatable level. He told me I'd need to meet with a psychiatrist before we could officially confirm a diagnosis, but to him it seemed pretty textbook: I was likely bipolar II (there were still some ceilings to my highs and lows). Because I'd brought myself in to see him at this pretty early stage, I'd probably be able to keep it in check with a relatively low dose of meds. (He was right.) And then he asked me if anything had happened: while I'd likely been on the spectrum my whole life, an event had probably acted as the catalyst to make my brain go from zero to 100. I told him about the night in my apartment when I felt like I'd broken; the night I couldn't stop crying and had felt such an all-encompassing sadness, that nothing in the world had ever seemed as big.

"Ah!" He smiled. "That was probably it, then. But we're going to get this under control."

I didn't know real relief until then. It felt good to have given whatever it was a name. It was an even bigger relief to begin to experience feelings with limits. Over time (and doctor's appointments, and blood tests, and medication adjustments), I started to know what reasonable responses to sadness and happiness looked like again. I began to know how to take bad news in stride and how to pause and ask myself if I was acting reasonably, or why I was feeling the way I did. I began to feel like a person instead of a canvas for emotional excess. And I even began to write about it.

I was finally interesting. But when you no longer have a choice in that fact, it becomes less story fodder than something you have to deal with. In less than a year, the magic of being diagnosed had begun to wear off, and my bipolar disorder no longer felt like a story hook. It felt like a part of me I wasn't sure I wanted to sit with anymore. So the further away I got from the diagnosis and all that had led up to it, the more I downplayed the extremes or made them punchlines I could use before anybody else could. I came to resent the head tilts and looks of surprise that go hand in hand with sharing what I'd come to see as a particularly unglamorous part of my life. If this was what interesting was, I didn't want it anymore. I hadn't counted on the most interesting people not being able to opt out. I didn't want to be the woman who does everything *despite* her bipolar disorder. I wanted to be the woman who has many complexities, her bipolar disorder being just one of them. (You know, a *person*).

After being diagnosed, I spent an afternoon desperately Googling "bipolar celebrities," hoping I'd find a person who'd managed to thrive outside the umbrella of their diagnosis. And I remember the joy of realizing Carrie Fisher wasn't just open about being bipolar, but spoke about it in such a candid, matter-of-fact way. I was in awe of the way her mental health was part of her story, but not the entire story. She was honest and funny and successful and smart, and she didn't cradle her mental health like precious cargo or her only notable quality. She was Carrie — a complete and whole person. She was interesting. On her own terms.

I'm still trying to write and talk about my mental health in a way that's comfortable for me. I hate being told I'm "brave,"

as if I had a choice but to play the cards I was dealt. I hate that at one point I was so willing to write and to share that I overgeneralized and overassumed and wrote pieces that were downright ignorant because I believed everybody who was bipolar had felt the way I did. I'm embarrassed that for a second between the relief of being diagnosed and the dread of it being brought up at a Q&A, I thought maybe mental health could really be The Thing. Sometimes I hate that I have to acknowledge it at all.

That's why my instinct has been to retreat, thinking that if I make the most complicated part of me invisible, I'll never have to deal with what makes me unhappy about it. But holy shit, so many things already make me unhappy. I don't need to wave a flag that reads "I have a mental health disorder!" (I hate flags), but I believe we should own our stories, own the way our mental health threads itself through our narratives. Even if you don't warm up to your story right away.

Not every story has to make everybody laugh. Not every story has to make everybody feel fine. That's what real life looks like: full of nuances and nonsense. At one point, we've all been in a metaphorical park, crying about not getting a text back. At others, we've invested in what we assumed would be a life-changing candle. We've all needed help.

We've also always been interesting, with or without a diagnosis or a tragedy. I wish I'd known I was always enough.

WHILE IN
THE AWFUL

You know when somebody starts a conversation by saying they've been "dealing with something" for a while and "it's been a tough year" and "the last month especially" has been a big one, and then they don't go into it, and you're like, "Bitch, are you serious?" Hello and welcome to real life. In our small section of the galaxy, many of us are dealing with things that aren't ours enough to talk about, but are still ours enough that we have to deal with them. Which is a weird thing when somebody asks, "What's new?" and you're like "UGHHHH," and then you follow that with "Oh, nothing!"

But it's fine. Everything will be fine. Or it won't! [*Manic laughter.*] This is the feeling I closed 2016 and 2017 with, which kind of fit in with everybody else's shit years. Towards the end of last year, I was texting with one of my best friends about what I was facing, and what she was facing, and she kept it simple. "Remember," she wrote, "it's okay to feel awful because everything is awful." And holy shit — what a comforting thought. It is okay to feel bad because things are bad. I know we talk ourselves out of moods a lot, and I talk about turning anger into productivity, but Jesus Christ, sometimes you just have to Feel Bad.

A lot of us are Feeling Bad right now. And that's because there's a lot to feel bad about. There's the big picture badness (climate change! tyrants in power! death by dysentery!), but then there's the personal badness that lurks in the shadows and threatens to change *everything*. You start to forget when your problems were like "Oh, I don't know if my crush likes me back." You truly cannot believe that any problem that could be solved with a single, simple conversation ever consumed you. You wish you'd known it was so easy then. You didn't know awful, and now you do. And you don't know when it's going to end.

Your patience is gone. And you resent people who aren't dealing with things of the same magnitude, and you don't know how to show empathy for things that are decidedly less dire. If somebody tells you how lucky they are that they've never really had any hard times or experienced straight-up fucking garbage, you . . . um, hate them? Like, how dare you not know what it's like to be swallowed by something appalling. How dare you experience joy without the footnote of "But outside of this brief, blessed reprieve, the Bad Thing is still happening." How dare you?

While in the awful, it is fine and acceptable to be like, "I cannot go to that party tonight because, honestly, I just don't want to be around that many people right now." It is fine and acceptable to cocoon and to admit that no, right now, you do *not* have the emotional bandwidth to deal with anything but The Thing. It is fine and acceptable to be choosy about who you can be around and talk to and commiserate with. All of it is fine and acceptable. Sometimes you get to be taken out of the moment, you get to be distracted for a second — and that's fine. As much as we talk about joy and gratitude and staying positive, we also need to talk about the value in being and feeling the opposite: you still have to go to work and eat your meals and be alive, but you are also allowed to exist in a realm where You Are Fucking Dealing With Something, So Fuck Off, Please and Thank You.

That realm can look like a lot of things. There's nothing wrong with anger, with sadness, with quiet. When I'm dealing with something massive, I don't revel in those feelings or exist there in that realm for attention or out of self-pity. I tend to push it down as much as I can, and I don't wear it on my sleeve. (Which is ironic, isn't it? I remember wearing the *smallest* shit on my sleeve in hopes that someone would think it made me interesting. Now, I'm just Erin Brockovich, yelling at everybody with purpose and feeling fine with it, thank you.) But I still feel it. And fuck, man — it's fine to feel it. Are things awful? Then it's okay to feel awful. Sometimes you can't think your way out of an emotional and mental abyss. That isn't weakness, it's simply being human and feeling things. Busy yourself with a rerun of your comfort watch and remind yourself that you're not being dramatic; sometimes things are just Not Good.

But they won't stay Not Good forever. Everything ends. And I mean that in a good way. Inevitably, the awfulness ends. And you will remember it happened, but the sting will lessen. And you will know you got through it, and you will get through the next wave of awful too. And when that happens, it's okay to feel awful again. And anyone who tries to talk you out of it can fuck off. Or tell me, and I will tell them to fuck off. Because while in the awful, telling people off is my favorite thing. I've got you.

THAT GUY™

Dating in general is terrible, but it's the worst as a teen. All things are heightened: you feel all the feels, you emote beyond your control, and all you want is to be wanted in the way Ryan Phillippe wanted Reese Witherspoon in *Cruel Intentions*.

I personally blame Leonardo DiCaprio. After watching *Titanic* no less than 11 times every day for 13 months, I'd become completely enamored and had to do something with the passion I felt for Leo. I transferred it onto a classmate named Liam, who, by the age of 13, had already burned down a townhouse.

Liam was complicated. He had ADD, took too much Ritalin on purpose, and at one point threw his desk across our classroom because why wouldn't he? But Liam was also tall and cute and had Leonardo DiCaprio's 1997 haircut, so by eighth grade I was understandably in love — which posed a problem. Burgeoning criminal record be damned, he was "dating" my best friend, Erica. Erica, knowing about my crush, had asked my permission before accepting his offer of boy-friendhood, and I had granted it. But it didn't stop me. One night over the phone, Liam told me he liked me anyway, and I lived for our secret conversations, peppered by me playing *Now That's What I Call Music!* on repeat in the background and asking if he liked the song "Crush." As far as I was con-cerned, Liam and I were very low-key in love, and I assumed (correctly) that we might even dance at eighth-grade grad. Nonthreatening boys and their kind, gentle demeanors could suck it. Liam with Leo's hair was my prize.

But phone calls and mumbled compliments at graduation are about as far as it got. From what I remember, Liam skipped out on grad early and left Erica in his dust, and soon after a three-hour phone call nearly got me grounded a few days later, he and I stopped talking.

Liam, to 13-year-old me, was a victory. I had "lured" him via my willingness to listen to him tell me about his problems while I titillated him with the details of the 3-D puzzle I was building as we spoke. Thus, he had ultimately proven to me that I was someone actually worth crushing over. The fact that he liked me (in secret) meant I'd won a very particular challenge. I was ready to date the shit out of every boy in high school.

I met Chad in the ninth grade and had absolutely no reason to like him. He wasn't funny, kind, or even interesting. He didn't look like Leonardo DiCaprio, and he seemed to care only about skateboarding, egging houses, and listening to punk music. He was loud, crass, and beloved amongst the hockey boys. But one of my friends had grown up with him, so we talked sometimes. And then at some point, something flipped: he decided to hate me, and I decided to hate him back. Of course, it wasn't a low-key, productive, adult type of hate: we'd go out of our way to be terrible, yelling at each other in the cafeteria, or I'd hit him with my school bag. We waged war over ICQ, at the McDonald's by my house, and in any shared public space. Chad was my enemy. Especially after he egged my house (and me), which he would do more than a few times while we were in high school. I hated him.

One night later that year, sitting at the park with my friend Lindsay, we started talking about how much I hated him, and she insisted that I actually liked him. I protested, suddenly nervous, thankful for the dark because I was definitely blushing. Because Chad would be a Real Challenge. Whether or not I truly liked Chad didn't really matter: I wanted him to like me, and that felt like the same thing. And if Liam had taught me anything, it was that I could win over someone who had burned down a house. So a guy who actively took pride in treating me terribly? I was up for the challenge. I could be a good enough woman to change for. I could prove I was worthy of someone realizing I deserved respect and kindness and, one day, if I worked hard enough, love.

And so began the longest six years of my life and the lives

of those who cared about me. Because the thing is, Chad always outwardly hated me. He made fun of me, encouraged his friends to do the same, and egged my house (again) on my 17th birthday. But when Chad was alone, he was different. On ICQ, he told me he liked me, but because I wasn't cool amongst his group of apathetic skater friends at our Catholic high school (or enough of a mean girl to make me a challenge in my own right), he told me I couldn't tell anyone. And then, after his admission of like, he would inevitably end up trying to date one of my friends and, in one special instance, invite me over on the condition that I bring her too.

But I was convinced I could change him: the perfect ICQ message or my new skate shoes would make him realize how good he could have it by dating me. Which would sometimes pay off. Sometimes, he'd tell me how pretty he thought I was over IM, and on good days he'd add me to his visible list, so I could always see when he was online. One night, he came over and we played cards. One afternoon, I went over to his house and we made out. *Eventually*, he'd want to be my boyfriend, right?

Because I certainly didn't have any real ones. In moments of telling myself I was over Chad — when he'd be cruel and dismissive for weeks on end, no glimmer of a *maybe* — I'd move on to a new guy who actually did like me . . . only to drop the guy in question as soon as Chad said "hi" in my general direction. I'd make out with whomever, casually rendezvous with a friend of his (who also requested I not tell anybody about us because he'd also be embarrassed if anybody found out), and make it very clear to anyone listening how much I hated Chad and wanted him to die. Which was a pretty easy story to sell: if we drank enough around each other, I'd end up yelling at him as he loudly made fun of me, and if we hung out in a group, he'd make sure to let everybody around us know how cool and skater I was not.

Six years is a very long time to ride the wave of this dynamic — especially since Chad and I only ever made out that one time in 2003. But emotions don't make any sense, especially when your worth is hung on the advances, or lack thereof, of a young man who gets off on treating you poorly. I wasn't in control of my feelings, but I was certain I could win this terrible challenge. I stuck around, I kept trying — it would all work out and we'd have a real story to tell the kids. (Like about the time he answered "Do I ever?" when I asked why he hadn't shown up like he'd said he would.) Even after he'd tell me he liked me, but not as much as he liked my best friend, who he then made out with on my bed (which I was also on at the time). Even after he made me buy him hair dye and apply it, and then tried jerking off while I was behind him, my dye-covered gloved hands in his hair. Even after he'd describe me in the most unflattering of ways to anyone who would listen, or after we'd scream across a party at each other, me jealous and angry and hurt that he wouldn't acknowledge me with respect in public, and him entitled and mean and unhappy.

But the thing I didn't realize was, I had laid the ground-work for a bigger pattern that threatened to define the rest of my life. For years, I kept my feelings about any decent man at bay. Close friends would know if I liked a guy, and I would swear them to secrecy lest that guy find out and discover that I wasn't cool enough, or hot enough, or whatever enough, and only want to flirt with me on the internet. And meanwhile, I began moving full steam ahead into the next tier of challenges: full-on unavailability. Believing I'd "failed" at "making" Chad like me, I threw myself into a series of regrettable situations: men with girlfriends, men who had to be "rescued," men with drinking problems, men who were straight-up shitheads.

"No offense," my friend Ashley said to me one summer, "but you really do have the worst taste in guys." I joked about being Carrie Fisher in *When Harry Met Sally*. I was the friend who made hilariously poor choices and whose announcement of a crush was met with "Oh, Anne, no . . ." I liked guys who needed lengthy disclaimers. I was the friend who called crying after begging a guy I worked with to leave his girlfriend (like he said he would) as we stood in the darkened mall parking lot. He didn't. None of them did.

And as my twenties wound down, I realized that even though it felt like my ego couldn't handle more failure, I still had to try. And that I hadn't been, really. As desperate and sad as I'd been, I'd been choosing the easy route: the most emotionally unavailable, the worst behaved, the men most in need of rescuing would never ask me for true vulnerability. They would never actually love *me*, never see my actual self, never see me as anything but a supporting character in their own shitty narrative. They were the heroes, and I was a plot point (if that). I mean, at no point would they ever even ask me about my day.

And through talking to friends and to my therapist and thinking on my own, I began to realize that I may hate emotions, and I may hate being vulnerable, but I would hate a lifetime of that bullshit even more.

It's strange the way your first relationships — or situationships — can fuck with you just enough to linger for years. Our relationships with these stories can be even more toxic and damaging than the people who inspired them. Because some idiot made you feel worthless, theirs is the legacy you've chosen to let define you, to gauge your merit by. Every guy morphs into *that* guy, and every "challenge" is another chance to fix past failures — as if the validation of another person would ever be enough. And it takes years for you to realize that you will never be happy until you let this go.

You can't force self-worth, and you can't rush emotional recovery, and you can't hurry through breaking patterns you've kept in place to keep you safe.

I still keep my dating cards close to my chest, but now it's because I don't like people knowing too much about that part of my life. But I'm not afraid anymore to tell everyone that I used to like a guy named Chad, or about our toxicity parading as flirtation and feelings. One time back in high school, I was mad at him and said that I'd write about him one day. "I'll make you famous and no one will even know who you are!" I typed dramatically on ICQ. He laughed.

I hope he likes this essay.

HOW I LEARNED TO STOP WORRYING AND LOVE ONE DIRECTION

Right now it's the end of the year, and everybody who's ever listened to Spotify is sharing their top listens and their favorite artists on Twitter and Instagram. Which, like, awesome, I guess? Some people earnestly love music the way I love back-to-back screenings of *Clueless*, and if that's what brings you joy, I wish you well. But *some* people just want to show off the reasons we should consider them cool/edgy/indie/authentic AF. I was getting annoyed at the relentless posts about top bands and go-to songs, but I realized it was because it felt like being forced into a time machine to my own pretentious past.

Once upon a time, I used to care about music. And, I mean, I care about music a lot now, but as a teen — shit, even as a

12-year-old — I cared about music to the point of embodying that infamous definition of fandom from *Almost Famous*. ("To truly love some silly little piece of music, or some band, so much that it hurts.") I made Spice Girls scrapbooks. I learned, alone in my room, the choreography to *NSync's "Bye Bye Bye" and tried to learn Spanish so I could sing along to Selena. And then I graduated to rock concerts when I realized music could also be used to (try to) make guys think I was finally cool enough to pursue.

My first real concert was Silverchair, which makes me sound a million times cooler than I actually was. I was 17, it was 2003, and I went with a girl who was barely my friend and a guy who was a complete stranger to me but drove us downtown in his cramped, dingy Honda. The only shows I'd ever seen were local, bands fronted by dudes I knew from school, and I was nervous about everything from drunken strangers to the venue to somehow being stranded in Toronto to the music being way too loud and permanently damaging my hearing. And then the band went on, and I was changed forever. (Ever . . . ever . . . ever . . .)

To start, frontman Daniel Johns was a total babe, so I found myself down the eventually very familiar path of falling head over heels for a guy in a band, failing to understand that charm and faux accessibility were part of the performance. But even at the back — the very, very back — of the sprawling albeit cramped Kool Haus (RIP), the music itself managed to trump the man in question. I heard some of my favorite songs played IRL, and even better than on the album. I bought a T-shirt, and I spent the following week listening to Silverchair's complete discography on repeat while telling anyone who'd listen that they were *totally* my favorite band.

And for a while, they were. But as I got more and more into music, I began spending actual time trying to find new bands, new artists, and shows to fill my nights. My relationship with music became less and less about the feelings a song gave me, and more and more about using it to make myself seem cool. Which, of course, is the *least* cool.

So, by my early-to-mid-twenties, I was an absolute asshole. "You don't know that band?!" became my nonchalant cooler-than-thou calling card. I'd attempt to mingle with musicians after a gig so I could tell everyone I knew that's what I'd done. (My claim to fame? One time I "grabbed drinks" with a band from England. I drank a ginger ale and was home by midnight. But goddamn, I clung to that for *months* and believed in my heart I'd made all of them fall in love with me. Which I hadn't.) As someone who'd never felt like she really fit in, I wanted to be in *so* much. When I became a music journalist, I figured that not only would I fit in, but I'd get to decide who else would.

The first two years I wrote about music, I couldn't actually fucking believe it was a job I got to have. I worked for $10/piece, for free, for CDs, and for books. I smothered myself in notes on who was up-and-coming, who was not, who was trying too hard, and who "deserved" coverage. I anointed myself an expert (I wasn't) who could and should make or break a particular act (woof) and became the worst version of myself because I was using culture as currency.

And, of course, I *still* didn't feel like I fit in, and by 25, I was burnt out. After what felt like infinite shows, countless interviews, and no offers to write the Canadian version of *Almost Famous*, I couldn't find it in myself to care anymore. I was tired and unhappy and in debt and mentally unstable and drinking alone. I said goodbye to the music industry. That part of my life was over.

Years passed, I found some equilibrium, and by the time 2014 rolled around, I missed how much music used to mean to me. I discovered I could once again listen to the bands that had defined my late teens and twenties. They weren't painful reminders of who I used to be, but the soundtrack to some of my life's biggest moments. I began to care about new artists and artists who seemed like they were trying their best, and I stopped dismissing pop music as a guilty pleasure. Instead of using artists as barometers of cool, I began to see them for what they were: sources of joy, ways to connect, both reflections of our culture and a means of shaping it. And I finally saw music itself as a gateway to discussions about politics and social justice and gender and sexuality, among other things.

We might all have our own tastes, but music should be something that unites people out of shared excitement, not out of douchey, insecure clique mentalities or holier-than-thou hierarchical nonsense. Music didn't sign up for any of that shit. (And I'm sure it would very much like to be removed from that narrative.)

So, I'm trying to tune out my own cynicism as people I know revel in their favorites. I'm trying to remind myself they're not always driven by self-aggrandizement, and that it's possible to be enthusiastic in a public way without snobbery. For the first time in a very long time, writing about music makes me happy. I'm not a tastemaker (gross), I'm just writing about what I love: Drake and Harry Styles and Bieber's latest haircut and *~what it all means~* for the industry. It makes me feel like a kid collecting Spice Girls stickers again.

I am always happiest when I love things. And when you begin to stop listening to pretentious blowhards, it's amazing what you make room to care about. So say what you want — I can't hear anyone over my Best of Britney Spears mix anyway.

ICEBREAKERS:

A GUIDE TO MAKING A REAL SPLASH AT A PARTY

Ninety-nine percent of the time, I don't want to be at your party. I want to put on a nice outfit, I want to do a lap around the venue, I want to be complimented on my outfit in an appropriate way (after posting it on Instagram to show what I am aesthetically capable of), and then I want to leave.

But sometimes you can't leave. Sometimes, because life is cruel, you will realize too late that you've arrived before all other guests, and now you're in conversational purgatory with the host and their midwestern cousin who has strong opinions about terrible things. Or you will misunderstand the invite completely and, believing it to be a "drop in, drop out" situation, you will arrive unprepared for a full-on dinner party where you will be seated next to someone who insists on calling movies "films." Once, I went to a "thing" that turned out to be incredibly formal and, in my nervousness, I explained to our server the specifics of why I can't eat mushrooms.

But not anymore. I'd rather wear my eccentricities (otherwise known as the reasons I'm not invited to a lot of things) on my beautiful sleeves because, in moments of being candid, of being unapologetically yourself, you will immediately find your people. Here are some topics you can bring up to ensure that you are the most interesting person in the room, according to you (and to me, who would hang out with you in a second if I overheard any of these conversational gambits).

GHOSTS

I love ghosts. I'm obsessed with ghosts. I always want to hear about the time you saw a ghost, and I want to tell you what I think about ghosts. Let's talk about movies (not films) about ghosts, and then use ghosts to segue into spirits. I want to talk about the time you're pretty sure you came face-to-face with a spirit, and I want to talk to you about how I feel nauseous every time I go into a place that turns out to be haunted. I want to talk about *Ghost Adventures*, *Ghost Hunters*, and *The Dead Files*, and then I want to talk about the scary type of ghosts versus the kind that just seem to kick around.

If I die (because I plan to live forever), I will be the type of ghost that shows up at parties and hangs with the guests who are interesting enough to talk about spirits and hauntings and everything I deal with in my everyday ghost life. And then, out of sheer appreciation, I will rifle through their bags and coats and take the coolest things because what are possessions anyway? I deserve them. I'm a ghost. And now, look: you have something *else* to talk about at your shitty party.

FUNERALS

Speaking of afterlife plans, why not just bring up the coldest, hardest questions: who wants to be buried? Who wants to be cremated? These are terrific questions! So what if they trigger a tidal wave of feelings re: mortality? And why stop at post-mortem plans — ask your fellow partygoers how they want to die. Especially since those of us with like minds have already thought this through and planned exactly how we wish to shuffle off this mortal coil.

Me? Should I decide to finally expire (although I cannot stress enough how much I refuse to), I will do so in a public space filled with people paying homage to one of my recently deceased enemies. And, in a final act of thunder-stealing, I will make everything all about me and eclipse my aforementioned nemesis once and for all. I will be very, very, very old and very, very, very well dressed, and, from the afterlife, my nemesis will be very, very, very bitter.

And then we will join forces to haunt the hell out of someone we dislike even more than each other.

MURDER

I have survived entire parties by talking only about serial killers. Is it appropriate? No. Is it upsetting? Probably. But why not use an occasion at which dozens of people are gathered to talk about what human beings are truly capable of? Merry Christmas, let me tell you about why you should call the police the second a man asks if you want help with your groceries. There are no meet-cutes, only predators. And yes, I check twice to see if my door is locked before I go to sleep every night, and no, I do not remember ever not being paranoid.

Alternate icebreaker: in old houses, I like to ask if anyone's ever died there. And then I offer to Google the address and the word "murder" to see what we can dig up.

PODCASTS ABOUT MURDER

Bridge the gap between interesting people and less interesting people by ushering them into the world of true crime via stories they can listen to while commuting. Not everybody can handle Ann Rule, and not everybody's willing to learn while at a bridal shower, a Christening, or a visitation (regardless of how on-theme it may be) that real psychopaths are so manipulative they're largely unidentifiable, so take baby steps. (And no, for the last time, I am not a psychopath.)

PODCASTS IN GENERAL

I'm just kidding, absolutely nobody wants to have this conversation. I have a podcast and I'm saying this, and I think I'm saying it louder than anybody else. So while we're here, here's a list of other things nobody ever wants to talk about:

- Your book
- Their book
- Any books that aren't about true crime or ghosts

- Why you think the ending to that TV series was bad
- Why you think the ending to that TV series was good
- Your band
- Their band
- Movies
- What distinguishes *films* from movies
- 99% of all music (outside of One Direction because Harry Styles is a safe topic for every occasion)
- What you're up to these days (the answer is always "nothing," and you know it)
- What you're working on now
- Who you're dating
- Why you aren't dating that one person anymore
- Your wedding
- Their wedding
- *Muriel's Wedding*

It's important to remember that you didn't invent music, you didn't invent weddings, you didn't invent vinyl, you didn't invent Toni Collette, and I don't own a single title from the Criterion Collection. Please stop blocking my path to the shrimp ring.

TAROT CARDS OR ASTROLOGY

But don't just bring them up by shouting either word into the ether and hoping one of them sticks (which I also like to do). Ask somebody what their birthday is, and then apply the characteristics of their star sign to their personality regardless of whether or not they want you to. This will go one of two ways:

1. You will be hailed as a mind-reading genius whose intuition will take you far in life and usher in an era in which everybody asks for your advice (and actually takes it).
2. You will be hailed as somebody who is very annoying, which means boring, nonbelieving people will never speak to you again.

Either way, the outcome will be a gift. At one party, as a result of this tactic, a friend brought out her astrology book and three of us just sat there talking about what it meant to be a Gemini rising (hi) or an Aquarius moon (also hi). Everybody else seemed to find it weird, but I don't even remember any of their names, so obviously, this was a very successful party and I have just proven my above point.

HOW MUCH YOU HATE PARTIES

Because sometimes all other tactics fail. And while I would never suggest doing this at a friend's party (should you wish to remain their friend), I will say that nothing bonds kindred souls like their shared hatred of a thing. My earliest and best friendships were forged through disliking the same people, disliking the same books, disliking the same movies. My adult friendships have remained in place because we both can't believe so-and-so is dating so-and-so, and why doesn't this party have any bread?

And, if you're really stuck, just tear out this page and bond over your hatred of everything I just said. "Can you believe this broad?" you will say, regretting having desecrated a book, even this one, for dramatic effect. Your new friend will shake their head in complete disapproval.

But that is how my spirit will be unleashed. And three hundred years down the road, at a party without murder lovers or refined carbohydrates, my ghost will be summoned to make it a party you will never, ever forget.

AN ANNE FOR
ALL SEASONS

I want to be someone who thrives during summer. I want to revel in heat waves, look dewy in humidity, and use the surfer emoji without irony. I want to go to parks. I want to post Instagram stories of parks. I want to tag the name of the park I'm at on Facebook. I want to eat fresh fruit and feel connected to our planet. I want to descend on a beach and not feel hyper-aware and uncomfortable about being around too many seminude strangers.

From May to September, I want to be more than just sweat and SPF 60 sunscreen. I want people I don't know to describe my hair as "effortless" instead of offering me hair elastics. I want shorts and T-shirts — instead of slacks worn in protest — to be my proud summer staples.

As a kid, I liked summer. But that's because as a kid, you're a lovely, hyper, freezie-bingeing idiot, not a grown-up who sweats fanatically despite having to look like a professional person. As a kid, you get to run around outside and drink from the garden hose to stay hydrated. You wear a bathing suit as clothes, sometimes to a restaurant, depending on how close to a beach or lake it is. And while you'd know to avoid the kiddie pool a friend's little sister had peed in, you certainly didn't worry about the consequences of using rocks to hold down a tarp you'd sprayed with water and planned to slip 'n slide on. At its best, blue collar suburban summer is grilled cheese outside on the driveway wearing water wings for no explicable reason. At its worst, it's being called inside for bed before the streetlights come on.

At the start of summer 2016, I was depleted. Paranoid that if I took a break — any break, even for lunch — I'd never work again. I'd surrendered to imposter syndrome and convinced myself that friends and editors were seconds from discovering how human I was. "What if?" became the first half of my mental call-and-response, the gateway to a million worst-case scenarios. I slept fitfully, couldn't eat without feeling nauseous, and still refused to turn down work or plans in hopes of keeping up appearances. Toxically dedicated to my performance as a perfect, godlike specimen, I told myself I couldn't be replaced if I distracted everyone from the fact that I was mortal. But eventually, my body rebelled against me. And within two weeks, I got two stomach flus and was forced to lie down and confront what would happen if I couldn't work for a while.

Nothing. Nothing happened. Nobody cared, in the most positive sense. Editors graciously extended deadlines, friends rescheduled plans, and all sincerely told me they hoped I felt better soon. My work wasn't reassigned, my friends still texted me back. As my physical symptoms began to subside, so did the cloud of self-doubt. So, with the Canada Day long weekend fast approaching, I made impromptu plans to road-trip to the beach. 2016 would welcome Summer Anne: a better version of myself who didn't recoil at the mention of fun. Or, at the very least, who would not feel guilty about taking a nap.

From the moment she took her shoes off at the beach and sat down on the sand, I liked Summer Anne a lot. She wasn't flinching under the sunshine, didn't worry about the way lake water could ruin the bottoms of her overalls, and she stopped using GPS halfway home so she and her friend could have an adventure. When the work week started, she began working on the stoop outside and learned to press pause long enough to pick up a sandwich for lunch. She still worked super-hard, but she wasn't defined by her work, which was new and exciting since it meant distancing herself even further from anxiety. She also began to use Regular Anne as a benchmark for what not to do: Summer Anne wore what Regular Anne wouldn't (crop tops), listened to what Regular Anne wouldn't listen to ("anything!"), and began looking the way Regular Anne hadn't (blond and very, very slightly tanned). Summer Anne did yoga.

Nobody wanted me to let Summer Anne go.

I sat across from my then-therapist at the end of August,

explaining the nuances of Summer Anne and how worried I was that September and colder weather and the inability to work outside would mean I'd have to kill her off. I was terrified of going back to the person I'd been, but more specifically, to the behaviors that had defined me. Summer has always been an excuse to cut work in favor of adventure; to laze around and to morph into cooler and more mature versions of who we were as kids. Autumn? It's textbooks, homework, and the reminder that we're all inching towards death.

"You know Summer Anne is just another aspect of yourself, right?" my therapist asked.

I sat, failing to absorb her words but pretending I absolutely had.

"You've always been this person, but you've just learned to tap into those characteristics."

She told me I'd always been Summer Anne, as if I could've clicked my heels together at any point and evolved into a person who didn't completely fall apart if she thought about meeting a friend for lunch. She made it seem like I didn't need to hit the wall in June in order to change.

But autumn that year was still weird. Normally my favorite season, its traditions felt dated, tied to the past of somebody I'd grown apart from. And while I used the underlying stress as a gateway into *The Great British Bake Off* and learning to frost cake like a motherfucking queen, I still felt stuck between the person I'd been in the summer, the person I'd been in the spring, and the person I was trying to be going forward.

Enter Winter Anne.

Winter brought wins, losses, turbulence, and influenza:

I was angry and tired and resentful. I condemned Summer Anne as having been too soft, too smiley, too receptive to feelings. I sneered at Summer Anne's "adventures" and green juice and petty deadline worries. Now I was Winter Anne, the embodiment of the season: a cold, icy motherfucker who should be feared and respected in equal measure. She got shit done because there wasn't a choice. She owned fur coats and had incredible eyebrows. She worked like her spring incarnation but refrained from hanging her worth on her work like her counterpart. She was her own advocate. She was a boss.

At first I thought Winter Anne had killed the others, that this was some kind of permanent evolution into my hardest, most unfuckwithable self, but I soon realized the other Annes were still lingering, ready to be evoked. Each Anne only ended the way books end — I could always return to them when needed. I could still set boundaries like I had in the summer. I could still be someone who baked her stress away. I could still be someone who could look a person in the eye and be cold and direct and terrifying. You favor the part of yourself you need to be at any one time, and you let the others hang back while you figure your shit out. None of us have just one facet.

Sometimes I still struggle to reconcile who I am now with the persons I was. But I also know not to worry, since whoever I am right now is exactly who I need to be.

BURN IT DOWN

I am tired and I am angry. But I am not tired of being angry.

I don't remember not being angry. I was angry when I became hyperaware that even walking outside as a girl could be risky. When I realized that guys could whip their dicks out at parties and women had to shut up and laugh or they'd risk not being invited to parties anymore. When friends told me about how scared or weirded out "beloved" boys at school made them feel. When I was asked about the status of my virginity every day by my 27-year-old male coworkers at my part-time job in 12th grade. When my coworker at the host stand whispered his sexual preferences into my ear. When a manager made me apologize to a group of men after I snapped back to their harassment. I was angry every time I was groped, catcalled, or told to relax.

But I didn't think I was allowed to be angry. As a tween and teen I blamed myself and I blamed other women for being sexualized in all the usual ways: for "asking for it" with their outfits, attitudes, or how much they had to drink. I dismissed gropes and unwanted touches and "baby" and "hey slut" as a reflection of the way things have always been. This was the trade-off for getting to grow up: your body doesn't belong to you anymore. It was my fault, because I chose the skirt, the shoes, the resting bitch face. I pushed my anger down to try to be a cool girl. I still wanted to be invited to the party.

Our society doesn't like angry women. They get called things like bitch. Like shrew. Like feminist.

After a friend from university sat me down for an extra-curricular Feminism 101 lecture in a coffee shop, I started to see the word as a badge of honor. I started to let my anger out. But I picked the wrong targets. I took my anger and hurled it at other women. I still blamed, shamed, and assumed my experiences were the norm. I didn't bother embracing inter-sectionality because I was too blinded by my own selfish anger to figure out what it meant. I believed that friendship equaled girl power and that women didn't need to show their bodies off to get attention, and I wrote that women in hip-hop needed to stop sexualizing themselves. (A piece I was deservedly dragged for — although at the time, nearly a decade back, I had absolutely no idea why.) I believed I could save the world with my #squad-centric brand of Basic Bitch vanilla feminism. And when I was called out, I was too proud and too willingly blind, convinced everybody else had it wrong because admitting that I'd made a mistake was too embarrassing. I wanted not to be objectified, to be recognized for my willingness to fight, but I still wanted men to want to fuck me and for any and all "cool girls" to applaud me.

I'd like to say there was an aha moment, but there wasn't. I don't remember when I paused to begin looking inward and to do my own homework and to learn to shut up and listen. But by my thirties, I began to feel comfortable with what felt like a new form of anger: a simmering anger that largely kept to itself lest anyone dare seek it out. And that anger wasn't directed at my fellow women, but at the systems and the people that keep the oppressed down. I was angry about what I'd believed as a teen, as a twentysomething, as a grown-ass woman. Angry about my own complicity in rape culture, in white feminism, in the exclusion of nonbinary, trans, and queer voices. Angry about being grabbed and prodded and privy to so many dicks I had never asked to see. I was angry about not enough people believing women — and angry that, at one point, I hadn't either. I was angry that I had defended shitty boys and men because I wanted to be in their favor, and angry that I'd eventually been disappointed and scared and saddened by those same men.

I was the person I'd been so afraid of as a teen. And I really fucking liked her.

When the Harvey Weinstein story broke, I read the accounts of his harassment, abuse, and sexual assault. And I was angry but not surprised. Because we've all known a Harvey — someone who wields power and keeps those below them afraid. I met mine as a teen. His name was Rick, he was a DJ, and he used his seniority to get away with a steady stream of harassment for months.

"When did you meet your Harvey Weinstein?" I asked Twitter. "I'll go first: I was a 17-year-old co-op student and he insisted on massaging my shoulders as I typed." I didn't think any more of it. And then came the responses. Dozens, then hundreds, and eventually thousands. Everybody had a Weinstein. Many people still do. My mentions became a tiny window into a massive fucked-up reality — but the silver lining is how this growing army of courageous, pissed-off people is connecting and together refusing to accept the status quo. One of the things that 2017 made crystal clear to me was that anger gets shit done.

So, I've come to relish that anger. It is the only thing I trust to fuel the work we need to do. I use it to defend myself (because heaven help the fool who sends an "actually" my way), but more importantly, to fuel my offense. It keeps me sharp and unfuckwithable. It pushes me to keep going, to keep speaking and sharing and helping reclaim space. But I haven't forgotten my misplaced anger either, so I also have to remember to shut the fuck up and listen sometimes. Because if I'm this angry as a white, hetero, cis, thin, able-bodied woman (Polly Pocket: Privilege), I can only imagine how angry women at the intersections of other forms of oppression are. Which means I need to connect to a larger community and movement, to let my voice be one of many, to be a voice that sometimes just amplifies other people's. Turns out this is great, though — because the only thing better than one angry woman is an army of them.

This world was created to make those who are marginalized and oppressed feel helpless. But helplessness is a waste of energy. What you choose to do with your anger is your choice, but don't ignore it, don't be afraid of it. It is not enough to simply seethe. You can implode the toxic patriarchal, racist, colonialist, heteronormative status quo through protests, petitions, or running for office. You can write, you can share your experiences or your art. You can take the time to learn: to listen, to read, to educate yourself. You can invest your time through volunteering or your money into an organization you believe in. You can create space in which real discussions are had, or engage in conversations that obliterate myths and shine light on truths. You can use your gifts, drawing on your anger to help you toil and dismantle a system that's been in place for centuries.

You and your anger are needed. You and your anger are valuable. You and your anger will be the fire that burns it all down.

GET TO
WORK

I'm a terrible diarist. I'll journal for about two days, realize how emotional I'm being over something that doesn't really matter, and then throw everything I wrote out and use the notebook for list-making instead because feelings are embarrassing, and I hate having them. Journals and diaries are where our most negative emotions go to die. And as comfortable as I've become (under protest) with being flawed and human, I would still rather be consumed by a plague of locusts than look back on April 2008 and my in-depth analysis of the way a guy named Steven said "hey" to me on MSN.

But over the last few years, I've realized a newsletter could be a journal that's not a disaster — that it could be a place to work through my stuff by zooming out instead of zooming in *Rear Window*-style. I write essays and lists that help me work through my stresses (without having to dwell on a particular person's tone on Twitter), and I vent about petty grievances so that I don't scream them out of my car window at innocent passersby. My newsletter has become my therapy — in addition to actual therapy — and the people who read it have become like pals. Which has been especially helpful as I've slowly realized that I won't die if I admit that I have feelings or slip into being vulnerable (sometimes). Over time, my newsletter has morphed into a place where I can be entirely myself — and where I hope readers feel like they can be themselves too.

Ultimately, it's the place I seek solace and remind myself that I'm not alone. And here's the other thing: neither are you.

For longer than I lasted at university, I've used my newsletter to write about writing, work, death, friendship, and the things I hate. But my favorite newsletters have been pep talks in the spirit of "Fuck you, let's do this." So here are the sayings (or yell mantras) I return to time and again, when I need some pep the most.

1. GET TO WORK

Right now. Get up and do the shit you need to do. I'm very flattered that you bought and are reading my book, but you need to put it down and do the thing you've been putting off all day. These words aren't going anywhere.

2. NOBODY CARES

Drink (or not, because Lord knows I can't) whenever I say

this because honestly nobody does. No one is sitting around dissecting that thing that you did or said unless you were grossly out of bounds and committed a crime. No one is combing through your Twitter feed or your Facebook photos or regaling their friends with the time you said "Hi!" really weirdly at the grocery store. Free yourself of the burden of thinking someone has made you the shitty supporting character in their life. They haven't. They're figuring out what to eat for dinner and freaking out about a typo in a tweet because, like you and me, they are also selfish disasters.

3. IT WON'T MATTER IN TWO DAYS

After the 2016 election, a tweet of mine got picked up by an alt-right blog and was shared a few thousand times between some names in that terrible scene. So, for the entirety of November 9, I was spammed with photos of myself along with comments as to whether or not I was worth raping. It was terrible, it upset me, and I hated it. But when I talked to my friend Scaachi, she gave me the rule I've passed on to whoever will listen: "It won't matter in two days."

And she was right. The next day the tweets dwindled, and the cold reality of Donald Trump being president eclipsed anything personal. It sucked at the time, but now it's fine. Also, the photo they chose of me was incredibly flattering, so silver: meet lining.

4. WHAT'S THE WORST THAT CAN HAPPEN?

The worst of all uninvited guests who insist on crashing your best-laid plans is second-guessing. So when the "what if" squad inevitably shows up, consider every avenue, every possibility. Pick up a pen and write down every single "what if" and then come back at it with a battle plan.

Like this:

"My friends will laugh at me."

Then they're shitty friends.

"I've never acted before, so what if I'm bad?"

You probably will be because no one is good at anything at the start. That's why you practice and take classes and join communities and practice some more.

"What if I'm fired?"

I don't know what you're about to do that merits getting fired, but here's what I figure you can be fired for: stealing, harassment, threats, assault, murder, racism, homophobia, transphobia, showing up drunk or high, setting fire to your work. Are you going to do any of those things? If not, go forth.

If you want to write, make art, start a band, bake? Things that don't seem like a big deal until you sit down and suddenly feel intimidated? You'll be fine. The only person putting pressure on you is you. Why would starting a newsletter or baking a cake or learning "Wonderwall" on guitar be anything other than a thing you tried? Last year, I tried to make something I saw on *The Great British Baking Show*, and I used too much butter and the oven caught on fire and smoke was pouring out of the stove and I had to call my dad, who put baking soda in the oven. And now I'm telling you about it here, so look: it's okay. Pick up the guitar and learn the fucking chords. Just don't bust it out in the middle of a party, or I will call the police.

5. YOU ALREADY KNOW WHAT TO DO

Most of the time you don't need advice. You know what you want to do, and you know what you're going to do, and, if you're me, you just want people to validate the choice you've already made.

Give your gut feelings more credit. You're not an idiot, and if you *are* being an idiot, rest assured we have all been idiots, in that we have all gone against our instincts at certain points. Whenever I have done something terrible, I've always known I was doing something terrible. It has never been a surprise that an act of self-sabotage or recklessness has ended in complete disaster. And whenever I've gone against a good gut feeling to make a choice that was safe or boring or a waste of everybody's time, I've known that too.

6. SELF-DOUBT IS POISONOUS TO YOUR WORK

Back in January 2011, I was very new to music journalism when I was assigned to interview a terrible band who made me feel worthless after sexually harassing me during an interview. Fun! Then, after that, a male journalist threw Nice Guy rhetoric my way, saying girls "like me" didn't like "nice guys" like him before insisting that, despite me arguing otherwise, I would want to have children someday.

At home, I panicked: why was I writing in the first place? How I could possibly learn to fit into a scene rife with misogynist Nice Guys quick to mansplain the politics of having a uterus? So I looked for proof that you could build a career amongst men who didn't give a shit about women. I found

Jessica Hopper. And, after reading as much of her work as I could without getting behind on my own deadlines, I emailed her about what had happened the night before and thanked her for helping pave the way for the rest of us.

She wrote back, "Self-doubt is poisonous to your work."

If my pain tolerance were higher, I'd have that tattooed on my every arm and leg. And while I never did learn to fit into that specific music scene, I did end up carving out a career that I'm proud of. Plus, Jessica not only became an editor of mine, but a good friend.

Even in those dark moments of thinking "Jesus Christ, why should I even bother?" you're wiser and smarter and stronger than your self-doubt and the place where it thrives.

7. FAILING IS FINE

I don't trust a person who hasn't failed. Failing makes you strong and resilient and wise and interesting. Perfect people don't exist, and the ones who aspire to be perfect are boring. Failing is how you grow. It's how you change and learn that you can resurrect yourself, how you learn to apologize, reconsider, and reject a life of self-pity. I have failed at retail work, school, finances, family, friendships, relationships, fashion, and driving my car. Today I failed at wearing an appropriate shirt to a blood test and had to sit in the clinic with my top half off while making conversation about the snow. I have learned that I don't know anything, and that I will never know everything, and that I will likely keep on failing.

But who cares? Look at how many times you've failed. The two constants in life are death and failure. (Hopefully, they're unrelated.) So yes, a lot of the time, things don't work out. But goddamn it (you'll say, vowing never to return to that specific clinic again), at least you tried.

8. YOU DON'T OWE ANYBODY ANYTHING

Okay, fine: you owe your family and friends something (like respect and common courtesy), and you owe your employers two weeks' notice if you want to quit. You also owe it to most people not to be a complete asshole.

But if you're at a party and you want to leave? Leave. On the worst date of your life? Get out. Someone you've never met on the internet is making their problems yours? Block them. At a bar and you no longer want to be? Be gone.

This is what I remind myself when I'm at an event/place/to-do/gathering/party/most things and feel increasingly like I really, really want to leave. So then I do, and nobody's bothered. The same rule also applies to: working for free, putting up with a person who takes advantage of you or your kindness, feeling obligated to do something you've been asked to do by someone with many demands who doesn't even appreciate it, and so on. You don't want to collapse like a dying star, so you need to take care of your brain. And a big part of that includes knowing when to say "Bitch, please" upon being asked to help someone you've met once dog-sit despite your severe allergies. No thank you! You owe them nothing.

9. KEEP YOUR EYES ON YOUR OWN PAPER

It's hard when so-and-so is doing the thing that you want to do. And it's worse when you realize you are rooting for them to fail because you're jealous. Jealousy is a terrible feeling. Jealousy is how we morph into the worst, most petty versions of ourselves (and inevitably why we end up owing a few apologies).

Never have I gone down the rabbit hole of creeping on somebody's work or life or Instagram and come away feeling good. I come away feeling like an asshole because now I'm even more behind on a deadline, and I know way too much about a stranger's life. But it happens, and we're human, and it's easy to think that if you can chart out someone else's trajectory to the top, you'll learn what it takes to be them — or beat them. Every time I've acted out of jealousy, I've told myself it was an act of control or reclamation. And every time after the fact, I've felt spectacularly unhinged and out of control.

When I was a music journalist, I used my bylines as social leverage. I'd drop the names of publications I was writing for to an acquaintance who was in the same industry because I wanted to remind them that I belonged; that I was a good writer who was worthy of being sent out on interviews or to shows *they* might not have been asked to cover. It was all bullshit: I was profoundly unhappy — broke and struggling, mentally and emotionally. Other people's accomplishments felt like personal threats because I assumed they were taking something away from me. I was defined entirely by insecurity and jealousy and spite. It was the worst.

Being jealous does nothing. It turns you into a person who's unable to feel genuine happiness, and tarnishes every accomplishment when it's used to measure your sense of worth on a made-up scale. You hear about a friend's promotion (in an industry that probably isn't yours) and feel like you will never venture past your existing achievements. You hear someone from high school is getting married and assume that you never will. You discover the guy you worked retail with in 2006 has a new apartment, and you sit wherever you happen to live and actively resent the space you loved five minutes ago. And feelings like this will always come up; it's just up to you to say "fuck off."

So, while I'd like to say you should just decide not to be jealous, and that we're all in this together so let's remember that and be best friends, I know that isn't realistic because jealousy is immune to reason and logic. This week, I went through a stranger's Instagram for a full hour, trying to piece together their dating history because I was threatened by how close they seemed with a guy I have a crush on. But then I reminded myself to keep my eyes on my own paper. If I feel myself slipping into a jealousy wormhole when I see someone else shining, I remember that to gauge my self-worth based on someone else's accomplishments is a one-way ticket to bitterness.

There's a scene in *Mad Men* that I love so much. Ginsberg is salty that Don didn't introduce his idea to a client and tries to reproach Don by saying, "I feel bad for you."

To which Don replies, "I don't think about you at all."

Be Don Draper. Which is the only time in history anyone has given that advice.

10. IT DOESN'T HAVE TO BE PERFECT
Nothing has to be perfect, other than brain surgery. (So to all brain surgeons reading this: I'm sorry. And good luck.)

Just getting through the day can be an achievement, so

expecting perfection is unfair to yourself and your work and your relationships (and even your hair). Mistakes are how we learn. Embarrassment is how we grow. Getting bangs is often how we scream for help. And if you are sincerely trying, you're doing a lot more than most. Effort trumps perfection every time.

And perfection is boring. There's a reason we were all obsessed with Princess Margaret after watching the first two seasons of *The Crown.*

11. YOU'RE NOT ALONE

You aren't. You are not alone in whatever it is you're facing. You have family, you have friends, you have strangers on the internet, you have the barista who was kind to you today. And if you do not have those, this is a reminder that there are people who will pick up the phone and listen should you feel entirely solitary.

Reaching out for help is terrifying because it means admitting that you're struggling, you're vulnerable, you're human. It is scary and awful, and I have faked choking on popcorn in a movie theater to distract everyone from the fact I was crying. I didn't want to wade into what was really happening, and I didn't want anybody to ask if I was okay, because telling the truth would mean pulling back the curtain on my carefully curated life-is-perfect façade.

But you aren't alone. And you can ask for help and still be tough as nails. Regardless of whether or not you were just crying in a movie theater. I promise.

IT WILL NEVER FEEL
THIS BAD AGAIN

I am bad at death because emoting in front of people I care about is a nightmare. I hate when people I love want to hug me and say things like, "I'm sorry," but I would hate it even more if they didn't. I hate the look you get when somebody finds out you've lost someone, or the way you're confronted with other people's grief while grappling with your own. I hate the way jokes are received with a "So I guess this is how you're dealing with it" half-smile grimace, or when it seems like someone is just waiting for you to fall apart so they'll feel useful.

After somebody dies, I want to cry by myself and late at night so that the next morning, I can blame my swollen eyes on lack of sleep. I want to shop for things I don't need and order $75 worth of Pizza Hut to eat in bed. I do not want to talk about it beyond the hard facts: this is what they were sick with, this is how they died, the funeral is at 11. Please don't attend; I don't want to have to perform for you.

But more than anything, I don't want to face a world without.

My nana died after a short battle with cancer when I was 17, and I wasn't ready to lose her. I was already an emotional teen, and my nana was like a second mom who taught me the art of bargain hunting, introduced me to Colin Firth via *Pride and Prejudice*, and watched patiently for hours as I performed the entire soundtrack to *The Sound of Music*. She made my Barbies tiny pioneer clothes the summer I was obsessed with *Little House on the Prairie* and made the best bacon and eggs I've ever known. Until she got sick, I'd been lucky in having existed for nearly two decades without having to witness the realities of stage 4 cancer and what happens to somebody you love when they're faced with it. She was given the news on a rainy night in October after months of misdiagnoses, and she died on Thanksgiving weekend the following year. During the months in between, she'd get a little bit better, she'd get sicker, she'd try new chemo, she'd get sicker, she'd get better, she'd be on the up, she'd be violently ill, she'd eat again, she couldn't anymore. And then she finally said no more.

She scheduled our family's Thanksgiving early, opting for the weekend before because she knew she wouldn't make it to the actual holiday. Miraculously, she ended up being up and well enough to hang out, laugh, watch old movies, and eat. I remember walking into her room and overhearing her plan the details of her funeral with my mom, and promptly doing an about-face. I walked back to the kitchen and poured myself a big glass of vodka. My grandpa watched me suspiciously as I dutifully poured in a splash of cranberry juice before retreating to the basement. I lay down on the floor in front of *Monsters, Inc.* with my little cousin who, now 21, remembers none of this. At some point before he and my aunt and uncle left that day, my nana told him she was going to be with Jesus, and he went home and tore his room apart.

Two days after our early Thanksgiving, she was moved to the hospice, and on a Thursday afternoon, I held back tears while giving her one last hug after spending most of my visit hiding out in her bathroom, trying to erase all evidence I'd been crying on the way over. Lying still in the bed, she quietly told me not to be sad for her, and I lied and said I wasn't, even though I didn't want her to die. I crawled into the passenger seat of our CR-V and cried all the way home. In the days after, I couldn't go to work, couldn't go to school, and could barely carry on conversations about the reality of her impending departure.

On Saturday, my dad called from the hospice to tell me she'd passed. He asked if I wanted to come with them to my grandpa's house, and, opting to turn off my emotions instead of processing my now Nana-less world, I informed him of my plans to go to a party. I wanted cigarettes and alcohol. And, oddly, I couldn't cry.

At the party, I chain smoked cheap cigarettes and made

jokes about being the next dead relative when my friends told me not to smoke so much. I stood around awkwardly, not self-aware enough to recognize that my grief was obvious despite my lack of tears. I hijacked conversations with news of my nana's death, unable to cry but wanting the void she'd left to be recognized. I went home around midnight and told my parents I'd go with them back to my grandpa's the next day. The real Thanksgiving Sunday.

I sat around while my heartbroken grandfather started giving her things away to my mom and her siblings, who talked about the upcoming funeral — five days away. I absentmindedly stared at more *Monsters, Inc.* with my cousins, clutching the *Sound of Music* record I used to make her play on repeat and wearing her watch, and drank more vodka, and only cried when I was by myself. Crying made me feel young and weak. I wanted what felt like this never-ending saga to be over.

Nana's funeral was packed wall-to-wall. And I cried hard and dramatically, completely unable to keep it together despite having known for the better part of a year that she was going to die. Death was the worst, and I hated the way it reminded me of how out of control I was.

But the older I got, the more death became a constant. Friends lost loved ones, my family lost friends, and my dad and mom put our family cat down after 17 years. And there were some close brushes: when I was 18, my dad went septic after his appendix burst, and that same year Mom nearly bled to death after a complication post-surgery. In 2014, my Grandma Donahue died after years with Alzheimer's, years of being unable to recognize me or my dad or anyone who loved her. And with every death, I taught myself to emote a little bit less, pushing the acknowledgment of loss down as far as I could, desperate for a sense of control over the uncontrollable.

I came home from the movies on a November afternoon to find out my uncle Bill had been admitted to the hospital. He had a pain in his side, he couldn't control it at home, and they were going to do some tests. I ignored the conversation I'd had with my friend Nicole a few days before — about how I had a feeling that something bad was going to happen — and told myself the tests would point to something easily treatable.

Obviously, that wasn't the case.

Bill and Dan, my dad's two brothers, have been my extended fathers since I was born. Uncle Bill, a retired captain of the fire department, and I spent our time going on adventures — visiting the fire museum he helped curate when I was a teen, road-tripping to Niagara Falls, or riding the school bus route he drove after retiring. Through my adult years especially, we met for eggs and bacon to talk about family, his photography, my writing, and mental health. A Virgo like me, Uncle Bill's capacity for scheduling and planning and multi-tasking was something I aspired to: he'd talk to me about my goals and dreams in a way that made them seem possible. Regardless of where I was — emotionally, mentally, finan-cially — he urged me to keep going, making it clear how much he believed in me. The last time we had breakfast, he told me how proud he was of how far I'd come. I thanked him and nagged him about road-tripping with me to Detroit. I'd begun to feel precious about our time together.

For two weeks, we were met with nonanswers about the pain in his side — his symptoms changed, his fever spiked, he was non-responsive to antibiotics. During the first week, I hung out with him in the early afternoons while my aunt and cousins were at work, and I desperately tried to seem in control, talking to nurses and doctors about what they were giving him so I could pass along any helpful information to the rest of the family.

Despite being stuck in a hospital bed, he was still so unequivocally himself. And while I'd been too young to spend much time with my nana when she was sick, I was old enough now to appreciate Bill's friendliness and how he managed to make nurses laugh while battling high fevers and inexplicable infections. I was also old enough to feel scared and frustrated and sad and exhausted, particularly because we still didn't have answers. On the Friday of that first week, he was sleeping when a bunch of his friends and my Uncle Dan and Aunt Sheila stopped by. I touched his foot and said goodbye before leaving, commanding him to get better because I didn't know what else to do or how else to help. He sleepily thanked me and told me he loved me, and I smiled as I said it back, desperate for him to sit up and tell me that it was going to be fine, that he was fine, that it had all been a mistake. That night, he went into the ICU with a fever of 106, and we all waited, believing that if he made it through this, he'd rally and escape.

And for a minute, he rallied. For another week, my aunt dutifully kept my dad and Dan posted with any and all developments. When they visited, hazmat suits were required to prevent infection. On Sunday, while I put up the Christmas tree, my dad told me he thought Bill would be back home soon.

The next morning, Bill died. I thought back to our last moment together, wishing I had said "I love you" louder, more deliberately, and maybe so purposefully that it would've made some type of difference. I hated that my last mental picture of him was not the vivacious, enthusiastic, energetic man I knew, but a sick, frail person who still joked around despite clearly suffering. I hated knowing he'd been taken from me.

Death is an asshole. Regardless of illness or circumstance or gut feelings, you are never ready to accept never seeing someone again, to have nothing left but last conversations and memories. You are never ready to be left with how sick somebody looked, or the way they stood up and hugged you despite how dizzy and feverish they were. You are never ready to exist without a person you loved and still need. Death is a constant, but you are never ready.

When my dad told me about Bill, I demanded answers. I yelled questions as though my dad had something to do with it and told him to ignore any tears should he see them. My mom offered me a hug, to which I coldly said, "Absolutely not," before closing my door and crying as quietly as I could. I picked fights with her all week. I went to the mall that night with a friend, told her the facts, drank three peppermint mochas (of varying sizes), and felt no need to cry until

I was alone in the car. And then I cried harder, thinking of the upcoming ceremonials, paranoid that my 17-year-old self would somehow hijack my angry adult approach to grieving.

But there is a canyon between ages 17 and 31. So although I'd been a sobbing disaster when my nana died, I'd spent the last 14 years growing into Donahue traits: humor, honesty, and dry eyes in front of strangers.

At the funeral home, church, and wake, I did what my Uncle Bill did best: talked a lot, joked around, avoided tears and spiraling into misery. Which worked since nobody in our family put their feelings on display that week. Only in quiet moments would we share amongst ourselves. My family and I took solace in each other, realizing how alike we were in our black humor, and how nobody outside of us could completely understand what we were feeling or why we'd rather make jokes about coffins than accept tearful hugs. We could acknowledge together how awful funerals are. If you're lucky, death can bring together everyone left behind.

The day after the funeral, I stayed in bed all day, ordered Swiss Chalet chicken, and watched a documentary series about serial killers. I cried for hours, but I still haven't cried in front of any real person. It's the only control over death I have. And I will take it.

Because death has continued to throw its weight around. Friends have dealt with it, family members, acquaintances. But while it's scary and awful and exhausting and terrible, it's also comforting to have accepted that death will always be there and will always rip out your heart. It doesn't get easy, and it will find surprising new ways of debilitating you. But what does get simpler is your awareness of it — the reminder that you have gotten through it before, and you will get through it again, and it will never, ever be as bad as it is in the moment you are battling through. It will never hurt the way it did when you found out, and the ache will never be as painful as when you realize those were your last words to them. It won't be as painful forever.

Death's cruel silver lining is that it forces us to reconsider life. It swoops in and reminds us there's one thing we can never control. But at the same time, it eliminates the background noise. When it shows up, nobody remembers your Twitter stats or your best nine Instagram photos. Nobody gathers in small circles talking about your impressive bylines or marathon times or how terrific you looked in slacks. You are remembered for how you made people feel, how good a friend you were, how hard you fought, how you made everyone laugh, how when someone was speaking to you, you actually looked back at them and listened instead of scrolling through your phone. Death reduces us to our most basic, our best, our worst. It couldn't care less about your Next Big Thing.

So, no, we can't control death. But we can control how we breathe, how we act, the type of work we do. We can control what we say yes or no to, control who we choose to surround ourselves with, control the way we make the people we love feel. We can decide to be kind, to try our best, and to be honest. Those are the things that outlive us. When we're faced with the harshness of how quickly someone can be taken away, we also see how we'll likely be remembered: as human beings who are far more than the successes and failures we tend to define ourselves by. After we're dead, we just get to be people.

HOMETOWN
GLORY

I'm from a city called Cambridge and an area called Hespeler, and I hated those things about me for a very long time.

I grew up a proud Hespelerite. My dad and his brothers were raised in Hespeler, their parents still lived in Hespeler, and most of my friends were bred to happily represent H-Town — by going to Shamrocks hockey games or by starting fights with the girls we didn't like from the Catholic high school I used to go to. Teen summers were like *Dazed and Confused*: we'd spend nights drinking in parking lots — or better, in the basements of friends whose Cool Parents didn't care. One year, inspired by the movie *Deuces Wild*, a few of us nicknamed ourselves the Deuces and documented dozens of mall hangs, dinners, and joyrides on a handheld camcorder. (And every day, I'm thankful that footage has since been lost.) I loved being part of something that felt deeply rooted in community, and I thrived on the town pride that defined most of our adventures. I assumed that I'd grow up and marry my high school crush, and we'd raise our kids to love Hespeler too. And while it seemed like a small-town cliché — not to mention professionally limiting — I felt content with my overromanticized ideals of friends growing up to marry friends and expanding on the world our parents built for us.

But my parents never built that world for me. Yes, they lived in Hespeler, and yes, my dad had grown up there, but neither pressured me to stay or to get married or to do anything but find a career that would ensure my financial independence. All they ever wanted was for me to be happy.

Soon after graduating high school, friends moved away to Toronto, to London, to Australia, and the group I'd hung out with in high school weren't really my friends anymore. Plus, I didn't want to date or marry anybody I already knew: most of the guys I knew had grown into lovely young men, but we certainly weren't romantically interested in each other. And the more I grew into the person I was becoming, the less I saw my future being defined by a specific part of town. So I decided to break up with Hespeler. And I started talking shit.

Feeling cornered in my retail work as a result of my own academic floundering, I began lashing out at my hometown and painting it as an embarrassing, intolerant, and small-minded place that demanded a life defined by white picket fences and limited dreams. I fueled myself with that brand of resentment, using it as a way to excuse my inability to find my own place and my own spot and my own future.

When I started university, I was at peak animosity. Seeing my hometown as a weakness I needed to parlay into a punchline before anybody else could, I accompanied my tales of Cambridge with eye-rolls and condescension, implying that I was somehow better than the whole populace while telling anybody who'd listen how my writing would take me far and away, where no one I'd grown up with would reach me. Friends who'd never heard of Cambridge or Hespeler congratulated me on "getting out" while I reveled in their understanding that I was obviously superior to the people I knew and loved. Sure, I had friends who still lived in Hespeler, and I had family who lived there, too, but none of that mattered compared to the narrative I got to write for myself. The one I would use to rise above them all.

Which, despite the fact that I was faking it, is a classist, elitist, and dangerous way of thinking. But at no point had anyone made me feel small about my dreams or told me I couldn't achieve something. Nobody had shamed me for being single or suggested setting me up with the only other person in the city who was unattached and/or unmarried as a means of fulfilling my destiny. Hespeler even had an arts community that likely would've been kind and welcoming if I'd chosen to join it. Instead, I chose to overlook the way it survived and thrived, and I focused on its inability to be like Toronto or New York, as if cities could just become that way. I told myself it was Hespeler's fault I'd taken so long to find my way. And now it was time for it to suffer.

So, shortly after I moved to Toronto, I wrote a blog post. After visiting home one weekend, I'd gone to a bar I used to hit up religiously and failed to have a good time. High on my belief that this meant I was better than every person that darkened its door, I wrote about it in a way I thought made me seem smarter and worldlier and worth more than everyone I'd spoken to that night. I wrote about friends' relationships, chiding them for being with the same people for years, and wrote about people I didn't like, blaming them and our inability to get along for why I'd felt so listless and unhappy during my teens. After I posted it, a friend commented, "We're not that bad," and I deleted her comment angrily, telling myself she couldn't handle the truth. I had moved to the city and didn't need their feedback or critiques. I was better than where I'd come from, and I took a mean joy in letting whoever was reading know it.

Of course, I was the only person allowed to trash my hometown. While friends who'd moved were free to bad-mouth Cambridge and Hespeler, it hurt when music journalists I worked with poked fun at my hometown. But, scared to look uncool or oversensitive, I rolled with their punches and told them not to even *bother* mentioning Cambridge. I laughed at their jokes and tried to absorb their senses of superiority — even though the more I did it, the bigger the pit in my stomach became.

And then I moved back. Poor and in debt and sick and sad, I moved back in with my parents in April 2012 and was forced to reconcile myself to what I deemed a massive step backwards. I told anyone I ran into that it was temporary, that I didn't know where I was going but planned an inevitable move stateside. I said I wasn't a huge fan of Toronto, and was reassessing my next steps. I said anything to cover the truth: that I didn't hate being home. I liked being home. I liked Cambridge, and I liked Hespeler, and while I still didn't want to get married or settle down there, I liked being close to people I really knew and who really knew me.

But I also believed that you were defined by where you chose to live. And staying home meant being stagnant, job on the internet be damned.

The thing about looping back is that it doesn't mean you're not moving forward. Life isn't *Super Mario Bros.* Sometimes you have to retreat, reassess, and rebuild. For me, there was no aha moment or specific falling out with a friend that prompted me to reevaluate the way I'd been talking about people I knew or the town I grew up in. That's because it takes an inordinate amount of time, therapy, reexamination, sobriety, and prescriptions to tear away your emotional shield. It takes rebuilding and accountability and painful realizations that you probably can't come back from some of the things you've said and done. But I remember one winter day, about two years after moving back, when I looked at my hometown happily, reveling in its history and its messiness and the way it's never been anything but itself. I remember feeling proud of where I was from because, like me, it was also scrappy and complicated and storied and had seen some shit.

They say you can't go home again, but you can. And while it won't be exactly the same, be thankful: neither will you. I've written about constants — about death and about insecurity and imposter syndrome — but one of my most important constants has been my hometown. It's been Hespeler, where I spent the best nights of my teen years and also the worst. It's been Cambridge, where I was awarded enough space to grow into the woman I am. The nights spent walking around, hanging out at the park, and sitting in various parking lots may seem throwaway as parts of larger stories, but they were the backdrops to real talks and problem-solving and emotional crises that shaped me. The friends I made are lifelong. And while we are not the same, and our dreams and lives are different, it doesn't matter. Friendship isn't about specifics. *Life* isn't about specifics. We are always the sum of where we've been and what we've done.

Last summer, a friend and I went to the Hespeler Reunion, a party that happens every ten years and takes place over a July weekend. My Uncle Bill emceed, and my Uncle Dan rode in the parade after being inducted into the Cambridge Sports Hall of Fame. I spent the afternoon with both of them, watching in awe as they shook what seemed like an endless stream of hands — of friends and acquaintances and even distant family members. And that night, I ran into almost every person I'd grown up with. I remember feeling happy and proud, relieved I was next to a best pal I'd grown up with, who could acknowledge the simultaneous awesomeness and ridiculousness of being catapulted back into the feeling that comes with being at a glorified high school reunion. But I still liked being there, running into former classmates I used to party with who were moms and dads or aunts and uncles or, like me, actively deciding whether or not to flirt with the person they'd liked in grade nine. I looked around the main street of my hometown, and felt proud to be part of a community who took recessions and economic hardships in stride. I felt proud to be related to my uncles and my dad and to come from a family with a lot of drama and even more grit. I was proud of the high school I'd gone to and of the teachers who'd pressed me to try harder (and of the teachers I'd resented enough to try and prove wrong). I was thankful for the people I'd grown up with, suddenly aware that I had always felt safe around most of them at parties (a low, albeit important, bar) and had learned the importance of respect through their own demand for it. I was thankful I'd worked at the McDonald's across the street from my house that was just a step from where everyone hung out in the parking lot. I was — and am — so, so thankful for Hespeler and so lucky it was where I got to spend my time getting my shit back together.

Last week, I moved out of my parents' house after five years spent fixing my life from the comforts of my childhood bedroom. I moved someplace close to the remnants of an old factory that my grandma and grandpa and great-grandma worked at, and my balcony overlooks the row houses three generations of my family lived in. I'm two blocks from my dad's childhood home and next to the hotel his grandma once ran. I am surrounded by history and by memories and by the imprints made by people responsible for me being alive right now. And while I'm not the same girl I was at 16, or the same woman I was at 25, or even the same person I was at the Hespeler Reunion (although I still have all the same clothes), I am the sum of those people and I wouldn't be here (or me) without them.

My favorite part of who I am is the result of where I'm from. And while the messiness of being alive has taught me never to presume to know where I'll end up, Hespeler — and the people I love who live and lived here — will always be my home.

ACKNOWLEDGMENTS

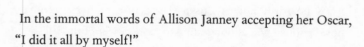

In the immortal words of Allison Janney accepting her Oscar, "I did it all by myself!"

Just kidding. (Like she was.) Mostly.

First, thank you to my agent, Carly Watters, who believed in me years ago when I pitched her the book that never actually got published. It's meant a lot to have you in my corner and to know that even when I was beginning to lose faith in myself, you kept it. Our lives have changed a lot over the last half decade, but I'm so happy to still have you in mine.

Thank you to Crissy Calhoun and Jen Knoch, who quickly morphed from my editors into family and therapists. You kept me together when coffee and fish and chips were my glue, and

I wouldn't trust anyone else to help me write about the best and worst parts of my life. Your patience, kindness, and willingness to listen have meant more to me than you could possibly know, and I still feel the same way I did when I first met you at ECW: *Holy shit, I get to work with these women?* We're friends for life now. Deal with it.

Thank you to Avril McMeekin and Rachel Ironstone, who combed through my copy to make sure I didn't sound like a total disgrace. You're as sharp-eyed as you are kind. (Read: very.)

Thank you to Jessica Albert, whose embroidery skills stopped me dead in the mall when she sent me the cover art. How dare you be so good at something I will never, ever have the patience for. And thank you to Natalie Olsen, who turned said embroidery into such a beautiful cover. It's super hard not to take credit for your work, and I resent you for having such an amazing eye.

Thank you to Susannah Ames for not running out of the ECW boardroom when I used a series of expletives to convey how serious I was about getting to work. I went full "I'll show you how valuable Elle Woods can be!" and you championed it. I'm sorry for how many emails I've sent and will send in the future.

Thank you to Nicole Villeneuve for being the first person to read this book and for making me feel like it was finally real and something to be proud of. I may not have siblings, but you will always be my sister. (Whether you want to be or not.) I am proudly the Dwight to your Michael.

Thank you to Scaachi Koul, who fielded my countless questions about book writing for months and held my hand through many small meltdowns. Your friendship and support kept me afloat through some hellish moments, and while I know you'll hate everything I just said, believe me when I say that I don't care and I adore you. Let's go shopping.

Thank you to Jessica Hopper, Emma Gannon, and Dolly Alderton, who were always very quick to remind me that it was natural to want to walk into the ocean after reading and rereading your own writing a million times. I owe you each many dinners for texting and emailing me back so quickly, and for creating work that inspires me constantly.

Thank you to my editor-turned-friend-turned-manager-but-still-friend, Sara Koonar. You've helped me remember to be myself and stop comparing my work and trajectory to anybody else's. If I could include a gif of Rihanna crowning herself here, I would. You are a true queen.

Thank you to the editors I've worked with and am still working with. You've all helped shape me into a writer whose work is actually readable.

Thank you to my grandpa, Antanas Laugalys, and my aunts, uncles, and cousins. Even when you had no idea what my job actually was, you've always been nothing but supportive.

Thank you to the Dell'Aquila and Franks families, who I grew up with and never let me think for a second that I should give up and quit even when I felt like an absolute failure. Erica Dell'Aquila and Catie Brooks, in particular: there's no one else I'd want to have survived Catholic school with.

Thank you to Sarah Hagi and Kiva Reardon, who forced me to get psyched about work and life and this godforsaken book, especially after casually flashing the cover art in a Chapters and saying, "It's not a big deal!" to your quite-appropriate looks of "What is actually wrong with you?" I love you so much, let's go eat steak.

Thank you to the friends who reminded me through all of this that it was okay to be vulnerable (ugh) and have feelings (terrible): Randi Bergman, Judith Ellen Brunton, Alexandra Donaldson, Sara Hennessy, Jessica Hobson, Ashley Kowalewski-Pizzi, Ashley King, Carly Maga, Sarah MacDonald, Amanda Brooke Perrin, Steph Perrin, Amanda Renaud, Alana Wakeman. I put you all in alphabetical order because I don't want anyone to know I've ranked you guys.

Finally, thank you to the staff at Starbucks on Hespeler Road in Cambridge. I would've perished without those lactose-free concoctions, and see? I *told you* I'd thank you in the book.

ANNE T. DONAHUE is a writer and person from Cambridge, Ontario. Her work has appeared in publications and websites such as *Esquire*, *Vulture*, *Cosmopolitan*, *Playboy*, *Nylon*, *Flare*, and *Rookie*. She is the host the podcast *Nobody Cares (Except Me)* and has contributed to CBC's *q*. You can absolutely find her on Twitter and Instagram at @annetdonahue when not baking or screaming into the night.